THE CANDIDATE:

BACK TO BUSINESS

BY

DIANA CARTER

THE CANDIDATE:

BACK TO BUSINESS

DIANA CARTER

Let's Do This Publishing

P.O. Box 301195
Drayton Plaines, MI 48330
ldtpllc@gmail.com

The Candidate: Back to Business

Family Drama/Relationships/Business

All Rights Reserved

Copyright © 2022 by Diana Carter

This book is a work of fiction. Names, characters, places, and incidents are the product of the author's imagination or are used fictitiously. Any resemblance to actual events, locales, or persons, living or dead, is coincidental

This book may not be reproduced, transmitted, or stored in whole or in part by any means, including graphic, electronic, or mechanical without the express written consent of the publisher except in the case of brief quotations embodied in critical articles and reviews.

LET'S DO THIS PUBLISHING, LLC
P.O. Box 301195
Drayton Plaines, MI 48330

ISBN 13: 9781733154888

All Rights Reserved

PRINTED IN THE UNITED STATES OF AMERICA

OTHER BOOKS WRITTEN BY DIANA CARTER

BROKEN PROMISES SERIES

Shattered Dreams
When Shattered Dreams Become Reality
Shattered Dreams The Final Chapter
In The Name of Justice: The Erica Blackstone Chronicles

DARK REVENGE SERIES

The Trey Taylor Story
When Time Runs Out: Tara's Quest for Vengeance
TJ The Forgotten Brother

THE SISTER FACTOR SERIES

Diamond's Fight for Justice
Dior's Darlings Daycare
Kristina's Kozy Korner
Krystal's House of Secrets
Never a Dull Moment: The Nick Jr. Story

UNBREAKABLE SERIES

When Two Hearts Become One
Unbreakable Deux
Unbreakable: Gracey's Redemption

THE MAKING OF A LEGEND SERIES

Neek's Rise to Fame
Desi's Drive to Survive

SINGLE TITLE

The Candidate: The Race to the Top

Dedication

This book is dedicated to a special lady that I've known less than three years, but she is awesome, Lois Ann Wiggins. Lois is the strongest person I've met over the last few years. She is compassionate, patient, and creative just to name a few reasons why she is an exceptional person. She has the ability to turn obstacles into victories. Her organizational skills are outstanding, and she has a great sense of humor. Working with Lois was great and now that she has retired I'm going to miss her dearly. What I've learnt from Lois has helped me dearly to deal with the quiet and busy times at work. Here's to Lois. May God bless you for many years to come?

Acknowledgements

The second book in ***The Candidate*** series was a long time in the making. ***The Candidate: Back to Business*** brings real life situations into the lives of best friends, Justin Bradley and Darius Kane. This book is a testimonial that you can't run from your past and what's done in the dark will one day come to light. Again as always I want to thank God for giving me the words, inspiration, and dedication to pen my nineteen book. Just thinking about this is amazing. I never expected to come up with so many tantalizing stories that could be enjoyed by young and mature adults. Whatever your reading pleasure may be, family drama, murder mysteries, romance, etc…this collection has something for everyone.

The last two and half years have been a challenge with the Pandemic disrupting our sense of normalcy. Will life ever be the same? Probably not. The new way of living is different, but society is coping the best way they can. As times change so will expectations of how people view the world. I would like to take a moment to thank and honor all the people in my life that stood by me when I was incapacitated for nearly three and a half months at the beginning of this year. The love and prayers received were appreciated more than can be put into words. At one point not being able to talk or walk was frightening. So to everyone that supported me from family to friends, employer to co-workers, and most importantly the hospital staff that gave me to reasons and the strength to push forward. I will remember each and every one of you with fond memories for the rest of my life.

God's blessing,

Diana Carter

The Candidate: Back to Business

Chapter One

Justin sat at his desk at the crack of dawn the morning of an important board meeting at WES. So much had happened over the last three years since he inherited the company. Every day he missed Ross. Ross Whitehouse was the founder of WES, his mentor, and dear friend. The first year was bumpy. He had to learn so much about the business in the short amount of time before Ross passed away. Working day and night, Justin almost missed the birth of his precious daughter, Allyson Anne (Allie). The pregnancy was rough on his wife, Alexis. Between the mood swings and crying spells, Justin didn't know what to do to keep her happy most of the time.

The next hurdle Justin had to overcome was a fight to keep the company. Six months after Ross Jr was released from rehab, Harrison Harper one of the men that ran against Justin and his best friend, Darius for the CEO seat put into Ross Jr's head that Justin had stolen the company from Ross' dad. It was rough going, but Justin was finally able to convince Ross Jr that Harrison was just using him to destroy him and the company. Justin was able to get Ross Jr back on his side. Shortly afterwards, Harrison left WES. The stress was too much for Ross Jr, so he ended back up in rehab. Justin received a call in the middle of the night two months later that Ross Jr had died from a drug overdose. This was shocking because all Ross Jr talked about was opening his art gallery when he was released.

Justin went through a slight depression after Ross Jr's death. He felt like he let both Ross Sr. and Ross Jr. down. He didn't have long to wallow in self-pity because there was a threat from a bigger firm to acquire WES in a hostile takeover. Fighting the company off put a strain on Justin and Alexis' marriage until they came up with the idea of working together. When Allie turned a year-old, Alexis realized it was time for her to get back into the workforce. She wasn't thrilled to go back to her old company, so Justin came up with the idea that she should come to work at WES as their Chief Design Office (CDO).

Alexis had years of design experience so Justin knew she would be a perfect fit for the CDO position. She was the head designer at her old job, so overseeing all the design and innovation aspects of WES was a good fit for her. A few months into his second year of business, Justin's best friend, Darius who moved to Florida to take care of his sick parents called to tell him his dad passed away then a month afterwards his mom overdosed on pills. Justin knew this hit Darius hard especially after losing Roslyn (Ross' daughter) in such a violent manner. Roslyn killed herself after trying to kill Justin and Darius at the press conference where Ross was going to announce Justin as his successor. Darius loved Roslyn, but she used him to try to claim the CEO seat.

It took a lot of convincing, but Justin was finally able to get Darius to move back to Michigan and to take a temporary position at WES (that's all Darius would agree to). But now over a year later, Darius decided to stay in Michigan, so Justin was going to announce Darius' new position at the press conference. When he offers Darius his new position, Darius was speechless. The new position would be Chief Communications Officer (CCO). Darius worked in this field when he was living in Florida, plus his old job at WES was similar.

Justin hoped he wasn't putting too much pressure on Darius. His friend had changed while he was away. He was calmer and more laid back, but he also seemed to be in a dark place. The CCO job would require Darius to be the head of all the company's communications and public relations. Darius has always been smart and a quick learner, but with the many losses he had suffered over the last few years; it had taken a toll on how he now approached situations in his life. Justin was happy that Darius had started dating again. Darius said there was no one special in Florida. He spent most of his time taking care of his parents.

Justin was so deep in his thoughts he didn't hear Alexis come into the office. She startled him when he noticed her standing in front of his desk. He still couldn't get over how amazingly beautiful his wife was after having three children. At forty-one she could easily pass for thirty. It only took her a few months after giving birth to Allie to get her hourglass figure back.

"What are you trying to do? Give this old man a heart attack." Justin said to his wife.

"Nope, not today. Maybe in another twenty years that may be a thought." Alexis said with a devilish smile on her face.

"Don't think you're going to get rid of me that easy. Now what do I owe the pleasure of this visit."

The Candidate: Back to Business

"I just wanted to wish you luck at the board meeting. I know I shouldn't laugh at him, but Darius is so wound up he looks like he is going to explode."

"I told him to chill. He's been handling the responsibilities of this position since he came back home. Today is just making it official."

"Well, I told Ciara to pop in to see him."

"Why did you do that, Lex?"

"Because she has a way of calming him down."

"I think you are mistaken. DK has been laid back since he came back home. That was one of the things I was just thinking about. I hope this title won't add undue pressure on him."

"I don't know what you are talking about, Jus. He was wearing a hole in the carpet when I left his office."

"We can't do much about that now. The meeting starts in twenty minutes. You want to walk me to the guillotine?"

"Stop being silly. This is a piece of cake for you."

"I appreciate your confidence. This needs to be the year that we make things happen. I don't want any other company out there to think that we are ripe for a takeover."

"You don't have anything to worry about, honey. After the way you shut Bloomsdale's down, I don't think any other company will take the risk."

"Enough talking. Let's go so I can get this over with. I have a busy day planned after this meeting." Justin and Alexis left his office to get to the board meeting.

Diana Carter

Chapter Two

Darius sat alone in the small room next to the conference room where the board meeting would take place. So many emotions were going through his mind. Had he made the right decision to come home? At times he felt that he didn't belong anywhere. Justin had a knack for making things seems so simple. He loved his best friend like a brother and still carried a lot of guilt for the way he treated him years ago when they were running for the CEO seat. Love can make you do some crazy things. Roslyn had him so twisted that he thought his life would be over if he lost her. That was the main reason he ran for the CEO seat.

Darius thought a lot about events that took place at the press conference. He knew that Roslyn was on edge, but he never thought that she was that far gone that she would go on a shooting spree. Once he was settled in with his parents in Florida, he had a lot of time to think about his life. His mom made him see that he needed time to heal. She told him he had a lost soul even before his relationship with Roslyn. He started dating six months after moving to Florida, but nothing serious. It was then he understood what his mom said about his soul being lost. He steered clear of dating within his race.

He brought the subject up to his therapist that he had been seeing for a few months. He didn't let anyone know that he was in counseling. There were times he wanted to share it with Justin, but he couldn't go through with it each time he attempted to tell him. He wrestled with how Justin was able to forgive him for the trouble he caused in his marriage when they was rivaling for the seat at WES. Darius came back to the present when he heard the board members gathering in the conference room next door. He planned on coming clean with Justin about his time in Florida. He owed Justin that much since he was going out on the limb appointing him CCO. His last thought before joining the others was, he hoped what he had to tell Justin wouldn't affect their friendship or his new position at WES.

Two hours after the board meeting, Justin and Darius sat in Justin's office going over the details. Justin knew things wasn't going to go smoothly, but he didn't expect to run into so many problems with Darius' appointment. Justin had two other prospects for the position before Darius came back to the company. Along with another interested candidate. These two employees presented the most friction. Shane Gibbons and Tucker Westbrook was dedicated loyal employees of WES. They were a great help to Justin when he was in the running for the CEO seat years ago. Then there was Kristen Carson. Although she had only been with WES for two years, she made a big impact on the company.

"How does it feel to be the new CCO at WES, DK?"

"Kind of unreal. I thought Shane and Tucker were going to have a breakdown. Kristen didn't take it too well neither."

"Kristen knew she didn't have a chance at this position. She's only been with us for two years. Our by-laws state that for this top position you have to have been with the company for at least ten years."

"You know what's running through her mind, Alexis. Since she has been here less time than Kristen, she should have been given special consideration."

"That's different, DK. Alexis not only brought years of experience with her, but she also brought exclusive contracts."

"I'm not saying it's a problem, but I think this is what going on in Kristen's head."

"Well, I'll be having a one-on-one with all three of them later this week."

"I better get out of here and earn my new promotion."

"I have to get back to work on that new proposal. Are you and Ciara still coming over for dinner tonight?"

"Yes, we are."

"Okay. See you later on, DK." Justin watched Darius walk proudly out of his office.

Chapter Three

Later that night Alexis and Ciara was in the kitchen putting the finishing touches on dinner. They had already set the dining room table. Justin and Darius were downstairs in Justin's man cave. The twins were down there too. Hearing the twins' laughter was a blessing to Alexis' heart. It had taken them a while to get used to being a big brother to Allie. Allie was taking a late nap. The boys were thrilled to have a sibling while Alexis was pregnant praying that the new baby would be a boy. When they found out they were going to have a little sister joy turned into disappointment. They were always coming home from school with horror stories from their friends how their sisters were getting on their last nerve.

The turnaround came when Allie had to be hospitalized for a week when she came down with a high fever that first started off with other flu like symptoms. She was only eight months at the time. The boys were not allowed to see her while she was in the hospital, so they became frantic when they thoughts their feelings towards Allie was the reason why she was sick. At thirteen, they wouldn't listen to none of the adults in their lives telling them Allie sickness didn't have anything to do with their feelings for her. The boys made both their parents pray with them every day that Allie was in the hospital. They promised God if He would make Allie better, they will never do or say anything to hurt her ever again. Alexis came out of her daydreams when she felt Ciara standing behind her.

"Girl, what are you doing, trying to scare me half to death?"

"I'm sorry, Lexie. I need to ask you a question about Darius."

"What about him?"

"I know we've only been dating for six months, but every time I ask him about Florida he shuts down. What do you think that is all about?"

"His parents' death hit him hard. I still think he's grieving for them." Alexis responded.

"I understand that. I do my best to give him space. What I'm concerned about is that he was there for a few years, but he refuses to talk about anything personal outside of his parents and work."

"Give him a little more time. Jus noticed the difference when he came back too. He is reserved now. We are not used to seeing that side of Darius."

"Okay. I'll be a little more patient. I just don't want any problems coming our way from his time down there. I'm also concerned about being the first black women he seriously dated."

"If you are getting at that he is not over losing Roslyn that couldn't be the furthest from the truth. He broke things off with her before she had her meltdown."

"Why do you think he likes dating outside of his race?"

Alexis quickly answered Ciara's question because she heard the crew from the basement coming up the stairs. "Justin says I'm wrong, but I think Darius wants a woman he can mold into his perfect woman. You know a real black woman isn't going to tolerate that mess."

"What are you ladies whispering about?" Justin asked as they entered the kitchen.

"Girl talk, which is none of your concern." Alexis responded with a slight smile on her face.

"You know what that means." Darius added.

"I do. It means they were talking about men." Jeremy said proudly.

"Go wash up for dinner and stay out of grown folks' conversations young man." Alexis said to her outspoken son.

After Jeremy and Jeffrey left the room Justin turned to his wife and said with a big smile on his face, "That boy is just like his mama."

A little embarrass by Justin's comment, Alexis responded, "What is that supposed to mean?"

"That he has a lot of courage and not afraid to say what is on his mind. That is a good thing, Lex."

"Whatever. You guys can go ahead on to the dining room. All your favorites are waiting there for you. Darius, congrats again on the promotion." Alexis said.

Giving Alexis a slight hug. "Thank you, guys. You have given me back the life I always wanted but was too afraid to step up and claim it." Darius replied.

"What are you talking about, DK? You had a high-profile position before you left for Florida." Justin was getting some strange vibes from his best friend.

"I realize that, but you and I both know that old man wasn't going to let my career elevate. He only put up with me because I was damn good at my job and to keep you happy."

"Let's table business talk for right now. This is your celebration dinner, so work is off limits." Justin said as he and Darius headed for the dining room.

Ciara moved closer to Alexis, "See what I'm talking about. Sometimes the things that come out of Darius' mouth doesn't make any sense at all."

"I'm with Justin. Let's celebrate Darius' new job and forget about the business or strange feelings talk until some other time." Alexis and Ciara took the last few dishes to the dining room. When the boys joined the men, they enjoyed dinner the rest of the evening.

The Candidate: Back to Business

Chapter Four

The morning after Darius' celebration dinner, Justin and Alexis arrived at the office earlier than usual. They wanted to get a head start on their workday before anyone else arrived. Justin tossed and turned last night. He couldn't get the talk he and Alexis had before they went to bed out of his head. This was the first time since Allie was born, they didn't agree on something major. Alexis was pushing Justin to have a heart to heart with Darius to see what was going on with him. She didn't want Ciara to be in another toxic relationship. Ciara's ex-husband was mentally, verbally, and physically abusive. It took Ciara almost two years to break away from him. She didn't want whatever Darius was keeping from them during his time in Florida to hurt her best friend.

"Lex, you need to lay off DK. He is finally getting his life back together. You had a front row seat on what crazy Roslyn put him through." Justin said.

"I understand that, Jus, but he hasn't been the same since he came back home. I know you see how different he has been acting." Alexis responded.

"He is still grieving his parents, Lex. He has done a bang-up job here since he's been back with the company."

"I'm not talking about his work. He has always had that under control, but not his personal life."

"I hope you're not going to bring up this race thing again."

"Jus, you know what Ciara has been through with that crazy ex-husband. I pushed her to get back out there. I knew even when she was still married, she had a crush on Darius but since she wasn't the right race for him, she tried to get over it."

"DK cares a lot about Ciara. There is no way he would intentionally hurt her."

"What about unintentionally? I think her feelings for him is deeper than what he feels for her."

"If that is true there is nothing, we can do about that. They are grown. Let them deal with their relationship."

"I need you to take this serious, Jus."

"Okay. I will have a talk with him this week."

"Thank you. That is all I am asking."

"Consider it done." Justin stopped Alexis from talking by giving her a passion kiss.

Alexis was about to leave Justin's office when there was a knock on his door. His executive assistant, Sage Browning came rushing in out of breath.

"I would say good morning but that will be a tall tale." Sage said.

"What's gotten you so up in the air this morning? Not to mention your early arrival." Justin asked.

"I'm sorry. Morning Justin, Alexis. I take it you haven't seen the morning paper?" Sage questioned.

"No, I haven't. We just arrive a little while ago." Justin said looking strangely at Sage.

"Well, I'm glad you are sitting down." Sage said as she walked across the room then handed Justin the paper she had in her hand.

Justin opened the paper and couldn't believe his eyes. The headline read, "Crazy to CCO: How WES' New CCO Landed a Dream Job. There was a picture of a spaced-out Darius on the front page.

"What the hell is this?" Justin finally said.

"I was shocked too, boss. I was having my morning coffee about to enjoy a little morning reading before I came into the office. I was shocked when I saw the front page."

The Candidate: Back to Business

"Thank you, Sage. Please leave us alone. Cancel my morning appointments and get Darius in here now." Justin was shaking his head not believing what he was seeing. Alexis took the paper out of Justin's hand then read the article. When she was done, she looked at her husband with tears in her eyes.

"You didn't know anything about this, Jus?"

"I don't want to read that garbage. Get it out of here."

"Jus, you have to address this before things get out of hand."

"I know. I don't want to know what that paper is saying. I want answers from DK."

"Jus, what are you going to do about this? We can't let this get out of hand. Who would do something like this to WES?"

"I don't know, but you can bet our last dollar I'm going to find out."

"Jus, are you going to be alright? I need to step out for a few minutes." Alexis said heading for the door with the paper still in her hand.

"Sure. I have to get my mind together before DK gets here." Justin watched his wife move quickly out the door. He laid his head on his desk and wondered what the hell was going on.

Alexis rushed to her office. She was going to call Ciara to tell her the news over the phone but decided she better see her face-to-face. It was a blessing that Ciara's house was only eight minutes from WES. She knew her best friend was probably just finishing her morning workout. Knocking on Ciara's door once she was let in at the gate, Alexis was anxious when her friend opened up the door with a big smile on her face.

"Morning, Ciara. We need to talk." Alexis said as she entered Ciara's apartment.

"Yes, we do. I'm sorry I was tripping last night. Darius and I had a long talked after we left your house last night. Then the hottest night I had in my entire life. I'm so happy right now I'm about to burst."

"Is Darius here, Ciara?"

"No, he left about an hour ago. He was going home to change then head to the office.

"I have something you need to see, Ciara." Alexis said with the paper in her hand.

"Okay. Let me get my reading glasses."

"I'm so sorry this is happening, Ciara." Alexis handed Ciara the newspaper. She watched her friend's face go from happiness to disbelief.

"What is this, Alexis?"

"Sage brought this in this morning to show Justin."

"I don't understand." Ciara said with tears rolling down her face.

"We are in shock too. Justin refuses to read it. He said he wanted to hear what Darius had to say."

"Why is this happening? We are so happy."

"We will get to the bottom of this, Ciara. I just didn't want you to be blindsided."

"Thanks for coming over, Alexis. I need to be alone."

"Okay call me later." Alexis left but the tears she had been holding back felled from her eyes.

The Candidate: Back to Business

Chapter Five

Darius couldn't believe the crowd of people in front of the WES building when he arrived at work. He wanted to get an early start on his first full day in his new position. When he arrived closer to the front door reporters rushed him asking him questions, he didn't understand because they were all talking at once. He figured the best thing for him to do was to get into the building to avoid all the questions that were yelled in his direction. Once he was inside even though it was early in the morning several of his co-workers were already there whispering in small groups. Before he could figure out what was going on, Sage ran up to him and grabbed him by his arm then ushered him into Justin's office.

Justin was sitting at his desk with a not so happy look on his face. He nodded to Sage to leave them alone. "Good morning, DK. Have a seat please." Justin said dryly.

"Man, what's going on around here. There are a mob of reporters at the front entrance and people are gathered in small groups in the lobby." Darius replied as he sat in the chair in front of Justin's desk.

"That's the question I should be asking you, DK. What's going on with you?"

"I don't understand. What are you talking about, Jus?"

"The mess has hit the fan. I need you to be upfront with me about what went down in Florida."

"We've talked about my time in Florida plenty of times. What is it you want to know?"

"DK, you're like a brother to me. Why can't you trust me enough to be honest with me?"

"Honest with you about what? You're not making sense, Jus."

Without saying another word Justin slid the paper across his desk that he had Sage to pick up until it was in front of Darius. All the color drained from Darius' caramel colored face. Both men were silent for a few minutes until Darius spoke up. "How did this happen, Jus?"

"We need to focus on the why this happened without my knowledge not how. I should have known about this way before now, DK."

"This has to be Shane or Tucker's handiwork or maybe both of them."

Justin was becoming more irritated the more they talked. "How in the world could you keep something like this a secret? I'm sorry, what I should have asked is if what's in the paper is true. Please tell me your side."

"I haven't read the entire article, but I can say that most of what I've read was blown out of proportion."

"I'm waiting, DK."

"This isn't easy to talk about. My time in Florida is something I wanted to leave behind me."

"As you can see that is not possible. You still haven't given me an explanation."

"This isn't the time or place to get into a discussion like this, Jus."

"You've took all of our choices away. If you had been honest with me, we could have gotten in front of this before all hell broke loose."

"I was trying to find the right time to tell you, Jus. My life here is finally coming into place. I just wanted to forget about Florida."

"What happen, DK?"

Darius stood then starting pacing around the room. "I'm not crazy, Jus."

"I didn't say you was. I need to know what is going on. You've just been promoted to a high-ranking position here, so you have to be above board about anything that is going to affect the company."

"There isn't much to tell. When I left Michigan, my focus was on my ailing parents. A few months after I was there, I knew it was time to deal with what happened with Roslyn. I was having nightmares about what happened at the press conference."

"Why didn't you mention any of this to me? You know I would have helped in any way possible."

"You had a lot on you plate already, Jus with the business, new baby, dealing with Harrison sneaky behind, and dealing with the loss of the old man." Darius never liked to call Ross by his name. He didn't like Ross any more than Ross liked him.

"You're family, DK. I would have been there for you."

"You couldn't have helped me much since you…"

"Darius, what have you done?" Alexis asked as she walked into the office.

"Lex, DK was just about to tell me what's been going on."

"Too little too late. I just left Ciara's. She is heartbroken."

"What did you tell her, Lexie?" Darius asked Alexis in a chilling voice.

"Hold on, DK. What's wrong with you, man?"

"I would like to know what your wife told Ciara."

"What you should have told her yourself." Alexis said becoming angry.

"Stop it both of you. What the hell is going on here?"

"Jus, I have to go check on Ciara. I promise to come back shortly so we can finish our conversation." Darius said as he headed out the door.

Justin looked at his wife and knew there was a lot more going on than what he knew about. He hadn't seen his wife so upset since the time when she told him she was pregnant with Allie. He was less than thrilled with the news since he didn't want to have any more children. Now it was Alexis turn to pace the room. Looking at his wife for a few minutes he had enough, so he went across the room to give her a big hug. At first, she let him then she pushed him away.

"What's wrong, Lex?"

"I tried to tell you he was keeping things from us. Now he's about to destroy our company and my best friend." Alexis said with tears rolling down her face.

"Neither of those statements are true. This company have endured more bad publicity than this and survive. As for Ciara, she will have to give DK a chance to explain."

"Why are you wearing blinders, Jus? He had no intentions of telling us what happened in Florida. This may just be the tip of the iceberg."

"We need to cut him some slack. Before you came in he told me about the hard time he had with the incident at the press conference."

Alexis was quite for a minute before saying, "That's fine and dandy, but he should have been upfront with us about this. We need to find out everything so we can protect our company and family."

"Stop talking like he is the enemy, Lex. He is family too."

"He has a great way of showing it. Now we got another fire to put out and he has only had his new position for one day."

"If you're getting at that we need to let him go get that out of your head. What we're going to do is find out everything that is going on and we are going to handle it without hanging DK out to dry."

"Jus, do you hear yourself? We need to find out on our own what's going on. He had over a year to tell us. If this didn't happen, he most likely would have still been keeping us in the dark."

The Candidate: Back to Business

"Why do I get the feeling you have bigger problems with DK?"

"I just don't want him to hurt you. You have always had his back, but this is something that could destroy our family and business."

"I'm not going to investigate him, Lex." Justin said sternly

"Why not. If you had given the position to Shane, Tucker, Kristen, or anyone else you would have done a detailed background check first."

"Lex let's table this for now. What we need to do is plan our next steps carefully and do some damage control."

"Sure. I'll have Sage to arrange for a press conference. It's ironic the person that should be taking control of this situation is the person that is causing it." Alexis said deflated.

"We got this, Lex." Justin gave Alexis a big hug before she left the room with a defeated look on her face.

Chapter Six

Alexis was glad that the press conference was scheduled for later that afternoon. It would give her a chance to catch up with Darius. She couldn't believe all the trouble that Darius was costing the company. Hell, he even had her and Justin at each other throats. She knew in her heart that Darius was hiding something since he moved back home. She didn't appreciate one bit the riff he was causing between her and Justin. All Justin could see that Darius was in trouble and as his family it was their responsible to help him.

Alexis was headed for Darius' office at first, but then she remembered where he was headed when he left Justin's office. She couldn't get out of her head the devastated look on her best friend face when she left her a little while ago. It was heartbreaking. Leaving out the back door where there were reporters waiting on statements, Alexis pushed her way through shouting at them 'No Comment.' When she pulled up in front of Ciara's house, she was right in her assumption that Darius was still there. He was parked in Ciara's driveway, leaning on the sports car he brought a few months back. Walking up to him with a determined look on her face, Alexis spoke quietly but angrily.

"What the hell is wrong with you, Darius?"

"I don't have time for this, Lexie. I'm trying to get Ciara to open the door so we can talk."

"Instead of coming over here to fill her head with more lies you need to take your sorry behind back to the office to clean up the mess you created."

"I'll head back to the office after I'm done here." Darius said harshly.

"So, you're just going to leave Jus hanging?"

"No, I'm not. You know better than that."

"No, the hell I don't. You should be there coming up with a strategy for damage control. That is your job."

The Candidate: Back to Business

"I don't need you to tell me what my job is, Lexie. What did you say to Ciara?"

"Ciara is the least of your worries. You have put Jus and the company in a vulnerable position. We have worked hard to fight off the vultures that has been gunning for us since Jus took over."

"I know all of that, Lexie. I just need a few minutes with Ciara. This will all blow over. We both know this is the handiwork of Shane and Tucker."

"Whether that is true or not, we have to get in front of this. You should have been upfront with us so we could have…" Before Alexis could finish Ciara came to the door.

"I need both of you to leave right now. I don't need you all starting trouble in my neighborhood." Ciara said sadly.

"Ci, we're leaving. We need to get back to the office to prep for the press conference later this afternoon. I will stop by after we're done at the office." Alexis said softly to her best friend.

"Don't bother." Ciara said then went back into her house.

"I guess you're satisfied now. It took me months to get Ciara to open up to me after her last breakup. Now you're putting her back in a space that she doesn't need to be. I'm going back to the office. I suggest you get your butt back there ASAP." Alexis headed back to her car but not before rolling her eyes at Darius.

Justin, Alexis, Darius, and three other executives worked hard the remainder of the morning getting ready for the press conference. They didn't have time to talk to Darius about the secrets he had been keeping from them. By the time Alexis and Darius returned to the office Justin was already working with the others. He only nodded when they entered the conference room. Alexis could tell that Justin was stressed even though he didn't show it. She was hoping they could have a little peace after they successful averted the takeover by Bloomsdale's.

The meeting got off to a rocky start. The other three executives were against Darius getting the position. Now they were sitting there with an 'I told you so' look on their faces. Justin had to fight hard against them to get Darius voted in. He knew at some point during the day he was going to have to have a serious talk with Darius. After they had everything in place Justin spoke up.

"Is everyone on board with what needs to take place at the press conference?"

The executive Ken who was Justin's right had man after Alexis said, "Sure, Justin. But we need to be realistic. We are going to have to face this head on and take swift action."

"That's exactly what we are doing, Ken." Justin responded.

"I think what Ken mean is that it may not be the right time to appoint Darius as CCO." Jack one of the other executives spoke up.

"If that is what he means then that is a moot point. Darius is our CCO. We are going to have to show a united front. Is that clear." Justin said sternly.

"Listen, I would like to apologize to the board. I didn't mean for any of this to happen. My life in Florida wasn't a piece of cake. I know I should have been upfront with some of the things that happened while I was away, but what we need to do now is to show everyone that WES is still as strong as ever." Darius said.

"We're going to have to deal with all of this later. I'll ask again, are we ready?" Justin took the nods from everyone as a yes then adjourned the meeting.

The Candidate: Back to Business

Chapter Seven

In a little over an hour Justin and his team of executive were going to have face the press with tons of questions being fired at them in which they didn't have sufficient answers. After getting everyone's agreement that they understood what their role at the press conference would be, Darius motion to have a say before they went their separate ways. Darius could feel Alexis rolling her eyes at him, but he couldn't let that deter what he knew had to be done. After all this had been his line of work for years and he was damn good at it.

"Justin, I think we should approach this differently. Can we discuss this matter between you, me, and Alexis?" Darius asked.

"If this is about the press conference the entire team needs to be in on what you have to say." Justin responded. Disappointed they were in this position so soon after Darius' promotion.

"Okay. We are making a big deal out of this when it's really just a few strategic moves we have to make."

"How so, Darius?" Justin asked. He could see on his best friend face that Darius was taken back with the way Justin said his name even though he called him Darius while in the office around others.

"We all know the press is looking for a fall guy in this situation. My therapy sessions in Florida is being blown out of proportion. Since I've been back home, I have performed this job in an excellent manner."

"Your job performance is not what's in question, Darius." Ken said in an angry tone.

"Not only is it my job to take care of issues like this, I think I should take the lead on this because I will be better equipped to address and answer the questions." Darius explained.

"Why in the world would we let you take the lead, Darius? If we had known about this, we could have approached it in a totally different manner." Alexis said letting Darius know she was pissed that his lack of honesty jeopardized the company.

"We need to hear him out. After all this is the job, we hired him to do." Justin interrupted.

"Thank you, Justin. First, I will take responsibility for what has happened. I can address the reasons behind my decision to seek therapy. We should answer the questions directly, but immediately following the press conference we need to create a press release to post on social media." Darius paused before continuing, "This will show that we are not only being proactive, but also transparent and accountable."

Ken spoke up again, "I don't know how this can be proactive. This should have been addressed before you were offered the position. You should have told the board about this before it became a scandal."

"That's water under the bridge, Ken. We are running out of time. We will give the press fifteen minutes to ask their questions. Darius will do most of the talking. I will do the opening then give the floor to Darius. You all have to be there but there is no reason for anyone else to speak outside of Darius and me." Justin said.

The looks on the other faces told Justin that they didn't like his plan. He knew he was going to get an earful from Alexis when they got home, but Darius got them into this mess, so it was his job to get them out of it.

The press conference was brief. The question were tough, but Darius field them like a pro. Justin had told the three executives to get back to work while he, Alexis, and Darius sat in his office to come up with the next steps. Darius was going to be responsible for writing the press release and posting it. Justin told him he would have to run it by the board before the post. Since the executives were gone, Justin decided it was time to talk to Darius like the brother, he always thought him to be instead of the CEO of WES.

"DK, what the hell is going on? You had plenty of opportunities to tell us about this. Why not be upfront with us?"

"I was planning on telling you guys soon. You have to realize how uncomfortable this conversation will turn out." Darius said.

"You know I love you, DK but now is the time to come clean about everything that may affect WES."

"Jus, man this is not a conversation that we should have at the office. How about we get together this evening then we can really talk."

"I can't this evening. I have to check on Ciara." Alexis said.

"I think that is best. I need to talk to Jus alone." Darius responded.

"No, that's not going to work for me. I get the feeling a lot more is going on here that you and Lex are keeping from me. We need to get this out in the open. Lex, I'm going to need you to check with your mom to see if she could watch the kids at our house tonight."

"That has already been taken care of, but I still want to check on Ciara." Alexis added.

"That will have to wait. We need to put all our cards on the table. I don't like the undercurrent I'm getting from you and DK." Justin said.

"Jus, do we really have to do this tonight?" Alexis asked pouting.

"Yes, we do, Lex. DK, we will come over to your place around five o'clock. We'll bring dinner. After dinner both of you better be ready to come clean. I have work to do. I'll see you guys later this evening." Justin started moving papers around on his desk and on their way-out Justin told Alexis to have Sage come into his office.

Chapter Eight

The trio had finished eating. Justin didn't like the things that were going through his mind. He knew without a doubt that his wife and best friend were keeping something from him. He was so disappointed that Darius didn't come clean to him about what was going on. He was ready to take the company in a new direction but now he had to deal with this mess. Alexis was sitting next to him still pouting because she didn't want to be there. She told Justin that she was worried about Ciara because she wasn't answering her calls. Now that Darius had walked into the room and sat in the recliner directly across from Justin and Alexis, Justin was ready to get started.

"DK. I'm at a loss for words. What else are you keeping from us?"

"Jus don't be like that, man. I know I should have come clean, but this situation is difficult to talk about."

"Difficult or not you had an obligation to be transparent." Justin responded.

"I couldn't find the right time to tell you, Jus."

"That's a broken record. You need to change your tune right now, Darius." Alexis said angrily.

"I don't need this from you, Lexie." Darius said just as angrily.

"Hold up, DK. Don't talk to my wife like that." Justin said. "What the hell is wrong with the two of you? Before you say nothing I'm not buying that."

"Jus, it's late. We need to get home to the kids." Alexis said in a low voice.

"We're not going anywhere until I'm satisfied with what is going on around here."

"Jus, let it go." Darius said in a calmer voice.

"I'm not letting anything go. You two have been hiding something from me. Lex why are you so upset with DK?"

"You can't be serious, Jus. Look at how he has treated Ciara. You know she had a bad couple of years."

"This is bigger than Ciara. I've noticed for months now that you guys have been tiptoeing around each other." Justin wasn't letting this go.

"Jus, let Alexis go home to the kids. We can talk all night if you need to." Darius said.

"No. I need to talk to both of you at the same time to find out what the hell is going on."

"There isn't nothing to tell, Jus." Alexis said.

"Well, I guess we will be here all night talking about nothing." Justin said stubbornly.

"Baby, please let's go home." Alexis begged her husband.

Refusing to say a word Justin looked at Darius waiting for him to start talking.

Darius shook his head as if he was trying to clear it before he started talking. "I was in a bad place even before Roslyn had her meltdown. As our relationship began to fall apart I was in the process of dealing with why my life was spinning out of control."

"Why didn't you come talk to me, DK?" Justin asked

"Man, you had suffered more than I had." Darius responded.

"DK, I need to hear more." Justin continued.

Darius continued. "I felt like I was drowning here. I needed to evaluate why I kept making the same mistakes over and over. I was also mad at myself because I felt like a fool for still being in love with Roslyn crazy behind."

"Can we move this along? We need to get home." Alexis said.

"I wanted to clear my mind with you before I left for Florida, but I was too messed up. When I got to Florida the days when I wasn't focused on my parents were torture. I couldn't take it any longer, so I started therapy. I didn't want to worry you or my parents, so no one knew about my sessions."

"I know I had a lot going on, but I feel like I failed you, man. You should have let me know things were so bad." Justin stated.

"I started feeling better once I found a job and got into treatment. Then when my parents died so close to each other I knew that I had to get away. When you offered me the job that was a perfect time for me to return home."

"I hear all of that man, but why didn't you tell us. You know how the press would spin all of this out of control." Justin said.

"Jus, we need to look closer to home. We know that Shane and Tucker is behind all of this." Darius said in frustration.

"That doesn't make sense, Darius. Yes, they wanted the CCO position, but they are loyal to WES. They wouldn't bring this scandal down on our heads." Alexis said irritated.

"No one else have anything to gain from bringing me down." Darius insisted.

"Are you sure about that, Darius." Alexis asked.

"What are you getting at, Lexie?" Darius responded to Alexis' angry comment.

"What about the women you messed around with in Florida."

"That has nothing to do with what is happening now."

"That's enough you two. We have to come up with a plan. Until we do I think you need to take a little time off, DK."

The Candidate: Back to Business

"Jus, I don't think that is a good idea. This is what you hired me to do. This is my job."

"Your job is to keep situations like this from happening, Darius." Alexis was ready to go home.

"Just a few days, DK. Lex and I need to get in front of this." Justin stood and helped Alexis up. "We will talk soon."

"Whatever you think is best, Jus. At least let me work behind the scenes."

"Sure. Why don't you start by thinking about the time you spent in Florida? I'm not ready to put this on anyone at the firm." Justin said as he and Alexis was walking towards Darius' front door.

"Nothing that happened in Florida followed me back here, Jus." Darius said with confidence.

"I would think about that before you speak so fast, Darius. Strange things have been happening to Ciara and now this. I'm getting the feeling there is a woman scorned somewhere."

"Alexis, that's enough for tonight. Work on what you need, DK. We will be in touch." Justin and Alexis left Darius standing in his doorway with a strange look on his face.

Chapter Nine

It had been two days since Darius had dinner with Justin and Alexis. He didn't like working from home but at least he was still working. He was extremely upset that he had hurt Justin. Outside of his parents Justin was the closet and most important person in his life. He had been through a lot of ups and downs in his life and Justin was there for most of them. For the first time since this happened he had time to think. What if Justin and Alexis were right when they said that Shane and Tucker wasn't behind what was happening at WES?

Darius was not worried about getting dress since he didn't plan on going anywhere. The press had the nerve to be camped outside of the gates at the condo community where he lived. His saving grace was after more than twenty calls to Ciara over the last few days she finally picked up. He was so excited that he was able to talk to her last night. What she had to say to him quickly dashed his hopes.

"Baby, I'm so glad you finally picked up." Darius said.

"I picked up to tell you to stop calling me and lose my number, Darius." Ciara said sadly.

"I need to explain a few things to you, baby."

"I don't want to hear anything you have to say, Darius. Has anything you told me been true?"

"Baby, I haven't lied to you. I just didn't disclosed things I went through in Florida."

"Wow, really. How shocking." Ciara said sarcastically.

"I've had some painful times when I was in Florida that I just wanted to forget about." Darius continued.

"How many women is included in these painful times, Darius? Wait don't answer that because I don't care anymore."

"Baby, please. Come over so we can talk about this."

The Candidate: Back to Business

"You got to be kidding me, Darius. Please stop calling me. I'm so over all of this."

"Baby, I can't leave right now. The press is camped out here. Please come over, Baby."

"Stop calling me, Darius. It's over." Ciara ended the call without giving him a chance to say anything else.

Back to the present, Darius knew he had to get his head straight because Justin was coming over later that afternoon. He knew it was time to come completely clean with Justin. This was going to be the hardest conversation he had in his life. He knew Justin would have his back if it didn't involve his wife. Knowing that he had to tell Justin some unpleasant news, Darius decided to have a few drinks before his best friend arrived.

Justin arrived at Darius condo a few minutes earlier then he planned. This was going to be a tough conversation he was about to have with his best friend. He knew whatever it was that Alexis and Darius was keeping from him, he wasn't going to like. He didn't like feeling like his marriage and friendship with Darius was in trouble. He gave both Alexis and Darius ample opportunities to come clean, but both said nothing was going on.

Justin was still reeling from his meeting earlier with Shane, Tucker, and Kristen. He had to get to the bottom of what was going on with this scandal. In his heart he didn't believe any of his executives had anything to do with Darius troubles. They were loyal to WES. They had been approached by several bigger companies to work for them, but they all turned the headhunters down stating they were satisfied in their current positions. The hurt on their faces when he asked if they had anything to do with the media circus told Justin all he needed to know.

"I know you all have an idea of why we are having this meeting." Justin said as they met in the small conference room next to his office.

"I surely hope this doesn't have anything to do with Darius." Kristen said in a stern but profession tone.

"I second that, Justin." Tucker said.

"You all know I have to get to the bottom of this situation. I'm approaching this from several different angles." Justin responded.

"I don't want to tell you I told you so, but I will." Shane added.

"Look, I know all of you were upset that I chose Darius over you all for the CCO position, but he was the most qualified."

"Don't forget your best friend." Kristen said.

"Yes, he is but that didn't affect my decision to promote him."

"Why did you want to see us, boss?" Shane asked.

"I wanted to get your input on this situation."

"My input is that I warned you that he wasn't being upfront with you." Shane answered.

"All I have to say is I didn't, and I don't think anyone in this room leaked this information." Kristen said assuredly.

"Justin, you are barking up the wrong tree if you think any of us had anything to do with this nightmare." Tucker added.

"Thank you all for coming on short notice. Enjoy the rest of your day." Justin dismissed the trio but not before noticing the sad looks on their faces.

Deciding it was time to go in to talk to Darius, Justin got out of his car then enter Darius condo when Darius opened the door before he could knock. "DK, you look like you been run over by a freight train." Justin said looking at his best friend.

"I've been busy over the last few days trying to think why all of this is happening."

"It is time for you to erase the most obvious off your list. I had a meeting with Tucker, Shane, and Kristen earlier. They didn't have anything to do with this."

"How can you be so sure it wasn't them, Jus?"

"Because they have been loyal to WES. They all had many opportunities to leave WES for more lucrative positions but decided to stay."

Darius sat down across from Justin at his kitchen table. I was sure it had to be one of them." Darius said scratching his head.

"DK it's time for you to come clean. I think this has to do with the time you spent in Florida."

"I'm not sure about that, Jus."

"I need you to tell me what's going on with you. Why didn't you reach out to me for help?"

"I was in a bad way and wasn't thinking straight."

"Tell me about it."

Darius took a deep breath before he started talking. "When I got to Florida for a while I was so wrapped up with my parents problems I didn't have time to think about the torment that was going on in my life."

"We talked two to three times a week, DK. Why couldn't you open up to me?"

"I didn't want to reopen the flood gate to what happened with Roslyn. When my mom seemed to be on the mend, and I had more time on my hands that's when what chased me out of town came flooding back."

"Why didn't you reach out then?"

"Because I knew you were still dealing with the old man's death. Then there was the huge responsibility of taking care of Ross Jr."

"I still could have offered you support, DK."

"I told you I wasn't thinking straight. Things had gotten so bad that I decided I couldn't handle it alone. The company I worked for directed me to look into their EAP. Swallowing my pride, I made an appointment to see a therapist." Seeing the look on Justin's face Darius continued quickly. "The first appointment didn't go to well. I couldn't open up.

"Why didn't you tell me about your sessions? You had to know that it was bound to come out."

"I thought about it when you offered me the CCO position. I figured you would do a background check. When you said that wasn't necessary since you had gotten a great reference from my employer in Florida, I thought I was in the clear."

"I bypassed that because I knew how much you cared about WES in the past even when Ross wasn't kind to you..." Justin stopped talking when his phone vibrated then answered the call. The blood drained from his face. "I have to go to the hospital. Lex is there with Allie."

"I'll drive you, Jus."

"Okay. Let's go." Justin and Darius rushed out of the condo heading to the hospital.

The Candidate: Back to Business

Chapter Ten

On the way to the hospital, Justin prayed that his baby girl was going to be ok. A lot was going on in his life right now, but all he could think about was Allyson. He still sometimes kicks himself for being such a big fool when Alexis told him she was pregnant with Allyson. He was in the fight for the CEO seat at WES and kind of gotten over the hump of the twins being older. Starting over at that time was a no go for him. He would never forget the look on Alexis face when he blamed her for getting pregnant on purpose. The sounds of horns blowing brought Justin back to the present.

"I don't know what could be wrong. Allie was fine earlier in the day." Justin said thinking out loud not really saying this to Darius.

"Lexie didn't give you any idea why Allie was brought to the hospital?" Darius asked full of concern.

"No. All I could understand through her sobbing was that Allie had to be rushed to the hospital."

"Try to take it easy, Jus. Allie is a strong girl just like her parents. Remember how fast she recuperated from her open-heart surgery last year."

Smiling Justin remembered how Allyson was ready to take over the hospital a few days after her surgery. "Yeah she was a holy terror."

"She is going to continue to be around to drive all of us up the wall." Darius said trying to cheer his best friend up then glanced at his rear-view mirror. "Man, I don't believe this. We have reporters following us."

By that time Darius had pulled up in front of the emergency room entrance, Justin said, 'handle this,' as he jumped out of the car and dashed towards the emergency room doors. Once he had gotten passed the information booth he saw Alexis and the twins in the waiting room. The boys ran to their dad as soon as they saw him. Alexis followed behind. They all hugged each other for a few minutes until Justin broke away to ask Alexis what happened.

"Lex, what happened?"

"Allie was sitting in her baby chair then she started sweating then she turned blue." Jeremy answered for his mom.

"You forgot to tell him the part that she started breathing really hard." Jeffrey added.

Before Alexis could add to what the twins said, Allie's pediatrician, Dr. Grayson walked up to them. "Justin, Alexis so sorry this is taking so long."

"What's wrong with my baby?" Alexis asked with tears in her eyes.

"Calm down, Alexis. Allie is in stable condition for the moment." Dr. Grayson replied.

"What do you mean for the moment?" Justin asked in a panic.

"We can talk about this in my office. Is there someone that can keep an eye on the twins?"

Jeremy answered, "We don't need a babysitter, Dr. Grayson."

"Watch you manners son." Justin said then continued. "DK is parking the car. I will have him to stay with the twins."

Both twins went to the other side of the room mumbling that they were old enough to take care of themselves. A few minutes later Darius arrived and agreed to stay with the twins while Justin and Alexis went off to talk to Dr. Grayson. Dr. Grayson was familiar with Darius because he was there with the family when Allie had her first surgery. After they arrived at Dr. Grayson's office and were seated in front of her desk, Dr. Grayson started to explain what was going on with Allie.

"Allison has a blockage in her valve."

"How could this happen again? I thought the surgery cleared up that problem." Alexis asked Dr. Grayson.

"I'm afraid we're seeing something different then what was previous done for Allie." Dr. Grayson responded.

"What does this difference mean, Dr. Grayson?" Justin asked. He wasn't going to beat around the bush when it came to his daughter's health.

"Allison's valve is not opening properly which caused her to have shortness of breath. When we repaired the mitral valve last year it wasn't anticipated that her aortic valve would become damage."

"Please don't tell me my baby has to have another surgery." Alexis said through her sobs.

"Yes, but this time it won't be the invasive type. We need to go in to repair the valve. From the test so far, there isn't much damaged to the valve.

"Allie has been fine up until this happened. How can she be fine one minute then the next she has to have surgery again?" Justin wanted to know.

"Justin we want to make sure that Allison's valve keep blood flowing in the correct direction through her heart. We are not taking any of this lightly."

"She is too young to have all of these problems, Dr. Grayson." Alexis added.

"Unfortunately, heart disease doesn't have an age attached. Just last week we had to have a newborn flown in to have a surgery similar to Allison's."

"What's next, Dr. Grayson?" Justin asked.

"We have to admit Allison then run a few more test. Once we get the results we are looking at thoracoscopic surgery. This surgery is performed by using long instruments that is inserted through a small incision in her chest. The good news is if all goes well she will be out of here within a few days instead of the week and a half she spent here last year."

"I'm staying with her." Alexis said.

"No problem. We already anticipated that. We have moved a cot in her room so you can be a little more comfortable."

This was the first time Alexis could smile. She knew last year she and Justin drove the staff crazy. "Thank you, Dr. Grayson. I want to let the twins know I'll be staying here tonight." Alexis replied.

"No problem. May I suggest that you guys take turns staying with Allison? She needs to know that both of her parents will be around if she needs them."

"We'll work it out, Dr. Grayson." Justin assured the doctor as she walked them back to the ER waiting room.

Justin tried to be cheerful when he told the twins, "Well, it looks like it just going to be the fellows tonight. Mom is going to stay with Allie tonight."

"Is Allie okay, Dad?" Jeffrey asked with a sad look on his face.

"Yes, son. She is going to be okay. She just have to stay for a few days so they can fix her up."

"Give me a hug. Don't give your dad any problems about your bedtime tonight." Alexis told the twins.

"I got this, Lex. I'll bring you a bag of things so you can change first thing in the morning." Justin kissed his wife, watched her hug the boys, and to his shock she even gave Darius a slight hug before Justin, Darius, and the twins left the hospital.

The Candidate: Back to Business

Chapter Eleven

Justin sat at his desk three days after Allyson was admitted to the hospital. He couldn't believe his baby girl was home already and tiring out everyone in the house. He and Alexis had a talk with Dr. Grayson the morning after Allie was admitted. After getting back all the test results, a procedure called Annuloplasty was performed on Allyson that morning. Thinking back to the conversation, Justin was so relieved that Allyson wasn't as sick as they originally thought.

"Good morning." Dr. Grayson greeted Justin and Alexis with a big smile on her face.

"Morning, Dr. Grayson. My wife was telling me that Allie has to have a procedure that should only take her a few days to recover."

"Yes, Justin. As it was explained to Alexis, Allyson aortic valve just needs to be tightened."

"Why did she pass out like that?" Justin perused.

"The flap on Allyson's aortic valve wasn't opening and closing properly. This caused a disruption of the blood flowing through her heart which in turn affected her breathing." Dr. Grayson explained.

"Jus. Dr. Grayson said that after Allie procedure she should only have to been here a few days." Alexis added in excitement.

"Sorry to cut this short, but if you guys don't have any other questions I need to check to see that Allyson is prepped for her procedure."

"We're good, Dr. Grayson. Thanks for keeping us informed on what's going on with Allie." Justin said.

"No problem. Allyson is our miracle child. We've never had a child to mend as quickly as Allyson from her surgery last year. By the way, we did a thorough check for everything pertaining to her heart. She will be good to go once we take care of this valve issue."

"Can we see her before the procedure?" Justin asked.

"Sure. Follow me." Dr. Grayson led Justin and Alexis to Allison where they were able to visit with her for ten minutes before she was taken away.

Justin came back to the present when there was a knock on his door. "Come in." Justin wasn't too happy to see Shane walk through the door and sit down in one of the chairs in front of his desk.

"What can I do for you, Shane? This isn't a good time." Justin spoke as he was looking through papers that were on his desk.

"I just wanted to express my sympathy for your baby girl. How is she doing?" Shane responded.

"Thank you. I appreciate your concern. She is doing great. Since I've been out of the office for a few days I have a lot to catch up on."

"I understand. I also wanted to let you know that I apologize for behaving unprofessionally when you made Darius CCO. Working with him over the last few days, I now see why you made that decision."

Justin was intrigued. He didn't expect to hear those words coming out of Shane's mouth. "How so?"

"Brother had a lot of flak thrown his way with the reporters and some employees getting in his face. He kept his cool then suddenly he had all of them eating out of his hands."

"Really." Justin said. Darius didn't tell him he had problems while taking over for him while he and Alexis were out for the last few days.

"I won't hold you up, boss. I just wanted to bring that to your attention."

"I appreciate that, Shane. Enjoy the rest of your day." Justin said then watched Shane as he walked out the door.

The Candidate: Back to Business

Alexis had just put Allyson down for a nap. The twins were a few doors down visiting their friends. She was trying to decide if she should take a quick nap since Allyson was a little fussy today. Instead, she thought she should catch up on some work around the house. She wasn't planning on going back into the office the remainder of the week. She had to be sure that Allyson wouldn't have any setbacks. The nanny was still coming by but instead of taking care of Allyson, Alexis had her running errands and doing other things around the house. She even talked her mom into coming over next week when she went back to work to help the nanny out. Alexis jumped a little when she heard the doorbell ring. She hurried to the door so that whoever was on the other side wouldn't ring the bell again and wake Allyson. She was shocked to see Ciara standing on the other side of the door.

"Ciara. It's so good to see you." Alexis said grabbing her friend and giving her a big hug.

With tears running down her face Ciara said, "I'm so sorry, Lexie. How is Allie doing?"

"She's fine. Napping right now. Come in and have a seat."

"I finally worked up the nerve to listen to one of Darius messages. When I heard about what happened to Allie, I was beside myself. I debated coming over or contacting you because I've been acting like such a nut case. I'm so sorry I wasn't here for you, Lexie."

"Don't worry about that. I knew you needed time to deal with all that happened."

"It's been so rough. I missed you so much. The final straw was getting a phone call from some chick saying she was Darius' wife and that I was a homewrecker."

Alexis was shocked to hear this news. She knew there had to be a mistake. "Oh my God. That can't be true. I know Darius has kept a lot from us, but he wouldn't keep something like that from Jus."

"I didn't wait to hear anything else. I stop answering my calls. I've been getting hang ups, but I started ignoring them."

"How are you really doing, Ciara? You look better than the last time I saw you."

"I'm hanging in there. I'm mad at myself for taking this out on you. None of this was your fault. I just couldn't deal with you seeing me having another meltdown from another relationship gone wrong."

"Ciara, you're like a sister to me. I will always be there to support you. It hurt like hell when you shut me out, but I understood."

"I know that now. I want you to go take a hot bath and get some rest. I will stay here and keep an eye on my Goddaughter until Justin gets home."

"I wish I didn't have to take you up on it, but I love the idea. I could have let the nanny watch over Allie while I napped, but I'm still a little overprotective of her right now."

"Don't give it a second thought. I look forward to catching up with you once you've rested. By the way where are the twins?" Ciara asked.

"A few doors down. They will be running in here around dinner time."

"Okay. I can't wait to see them. I missed all of you so much."

"They will be happy to see you too, Ciara."

"Ditto. Now go pamper yourself." Ciara watched her friend drag herself up the stairs. She prayed they all will be back to normal soon.

The Candidate: Back to Business

Chapter Twelve

Justin was packing up to leave the office a few hours after his meeting with Shane. He knew he had been right. Shane didn't have anything to do with the mess that WES was now facing. He didn't feel that Tucker or Kristen was involved neither. There was something bigger going on here. Once he was sure that Allyson was out of the woods he was going to have to have a talk with Darius to get to the bottom of their crisis. He wanted to hurry home. Alexis wasn't answering her phone when he called to check on Allyson. He knew the twins were down the street, so he tried to have them to go check on their mom, they didn't answer neither. As soon as he closed his briefcase his cell phone rang.

"Hey babe. You had me worried. I was just heading home." Justin said into the phone when he saw his wife's beautiful face appear.

"Hi, Justin. Lexie is sleeping right now." Ciara said.

Justin was surprised to hear Ciara's voice. Alexis had been worried sick when Ciara refused to talk to her after her relationship with Darius went astray. "Ciara, how have you been?"

"Getting better every day. Justin, I'm so sorry I wasn't with the family when you guys was going through so much with Allie." Ciara said with sadness in her voice.

"There is no need to apologize. We were all thrown for a loop."

"Even more now than ever. Did your dear friend tell you he was married?"

Shock spread across Justin's face. "What are you talking about, Ciara?" He had to have heard her wrong.

"His wife has been hounding me. She said I was a homewrecker and should be ashamed of myself."

"Somebody been lying to you, Ciara. DK isn't married."

"Are you sure about that. Justin?" Ciara asked.

Before Justin could answer, Darius knocked briefly on his door before entering.

"Jus, I know you wanted this report today…"

"I have to go. Tell Lex I will be there shortly when she wakes up." Justin disconnected his cell phone and sat back in his chair dazed.

"What's up, Jus. Is Allie okay?" Darius asked his friend with concern in his voice.

"DK, this can't be put off any longer. I need you to tell me what is going on with you. What happened in Florida, man?" Justin was so weary with trying to deal with this mess.

"We can talk about that at another time. I know you want to get home to Lexie and the kids." Darius said with concern for his best friend.

"No, this has been put off long enough. That was Ciara on the phone. She is at the house with Lex."

"Wow. I wished you would have let me talk to her. I've been leaving messages for her, but she hasn't returned any of my calls."

"Do you really think she is going to just wake up one day and you guys will go back to what you used to have?" Justin asked.

"No, I know it won't be that easy. I just want to explain to her that things are not what they appear."

"Explain it to me, DK. This conversation is long overdue."

"Why are you so upset, Jus? You don't like how I've handled things while you were away?"

"This has nothing to do with that, DK. I need to know what happened in Florida that has come back to bite us in the butt."

"Long story short, Jus. I was in a bad way when I left here. The stress of my parents' illness was another burden that was hard to handle. As

I told you, I started counseling. It was going okay for the first few months, but things changed, and I had to end my sessions."

"What changed, DK? You've been saying this for a while now without explaining." Justin asked.

"My therapist became unprofessional, so I cut ties with her, or I should say I tried to cut ties with her."

"So, what happened?"

"We crossed the line during one of my sessions. It only happened once, but she didn't want to leave it at that. After I stopped seeing her she began to stalk me."

"DK be honest with me. Is this all the happened between the two of you?"

"Yes. I swear to you, Jus. That lady was crazy. I thought no one would be as insane as Roslyn, but I was wrong."

"Were you involved with anyone else while you were there?"

"No. I was too messed up with what was going on with her."

Justin decided it was time to tell Darius about the conversation he had with Ciara. "DK, Ciara was blown away when she was accused of being a homewrecker."

"Homewrecker. What are you talking about, Jus?"

"She said that she has been getting harassing calls from a nutcase telling her she was your wife, and that Ciara was breaking up her home."

"This can't be happening. I know you don't think I'm married, Jus?"

"I just want you to be straight with me, DK." Justin responded.

Shaking his head to clear it, Darius said, "I know she's not taking things this far. Jus, I'm not married. I've told you she was the only woman

I been with when I was there outside of a few dates. I spent most of my time trying to avoid any interactions with her."

"Did you go to the police?"

"No. Once I decided I was coming back home, I just wanted to put all of this behind me."

"Are you thinking what I'm thinking?" Justin asked his best friend.

"If she is the one that is harassing Ciara, she is capable of anything."

"I'm going to call Ciara to see if she could stay the night with Lex. We have to get to the bottom of this. I need you to tell me everything you know about this woman."

"I can't believe she would go this far. I didn't want to get her in trouble, so I did my best to cut all ties with her instead of contacting the police."

"If she is responsible for this mess at work and harassing Ciara this woman is dangerous." Justin said concerned about Ciara's safety.

"Jus, I'm so sorry. I must have some kind of stupid radar that attract crazy."

"No, you don't. Ciara cared for you deeply. We have to get this situation under control. We need to find out where she is living. My gut feeling is telling me that she followed you back here and that she wants revenge."

"Revenge for what? I didn't do anything to her crazy behind. God, I knew I should have gotten a male therapist." Darius said with defeat running through his entire body.

"Don't worry. We will take care of this once and for all."

The Candidate: Back to Business

Chapter Thirteen

The last few days had been rough for Justin and Darius. Justin contacted the chief of police that was a buddy of his thanks to Ross to see what could be done about the craziness that has been happening over the last few months. Alexis was able to convince Ciara to move in with them for a little while until they could find out the whereabouts of the lady of the hour, Dr. Skylar Stevens. Justin wished he could forget he ever heard that name. He and Darius went down to the police station the same night after Darius told Justin everything that happened between him and the good doctor.

As he sat at his desk waiting on Darius and Alexis to show up for a brief meeting, he thought about what happened when they went to the police station. He was blown away when he found out that there wasn't much they could do from a legal standpoint since neither Justin nor Darius could give them any evidence that Skylar was behind their recent problems. Justin was more upset for Darius then himself when they left the police station because of the defeated look that was on his best friend's face. Justin thought back to their conversation with sadness.

"DK don't look so defeated. This is just the beginning. Rick is going to look into this for us." Justin shortened the name of Chief Erick Emerson.

"But how long is that going to take? We don't even know if that crazy heifer is here on not."

"No, we don't, but Rick will find out. He isn't going to let too much time pass before he gives us some answers.

"It's not just that. I feel like a teenager again wondering what the girl of my dreams has to say to me. I haven't communicated with Ciara for a good while, but now all of the sudden she wants to talk to me."

"That could be a good thing, DK. Maybe she is ready to discuss your relationship. You two were good together."

"I hate all the drama I've brought into her life. All I wanted to do is to give her peace of mind and the loving care she deserves."

"Somewhere deep inside of Ciara knows that. You know the saying 'it's hard to relate to a good man after you've had a bad one' or something like that."

"I guess we better head to your house to get this over with. I feel I need to stay far away from Ciara until we find out what's going on with Sky."

"Let's go. But I don't' think that is going to help, because you've haven't seen Ciara for a while now, but things are still happening to her."

Justin came back to the present when Alexis and Darius walked through the door. He was so happy to see that they were more comfortable around each other now. It didn't stop Alexis from letting Darius have it for bringing crazy in their lives, but Justin could see that Alexis wasn't angry with Darius any longer.

"I'm not going to keep you guys for long. I just wanted to let both of you know that Rick will come over to the house later this evening. I've already arranged for your mom to keep the kids for tonight."

"Jus, why do the kids have to stay overnight? It is too soon for Allie to have overnight stays." Alexis asked her husband.

"Lex, we need to get to the bottom of this. Plus, I thought it would be good for us after everyone left to have some alone time. Ciara is going to be at the meeting since this concerns her, but she will be going over to her sister's for a few days."

"I think she should stay with us. You know she doesn't get along with that drama queen."

Speaking for the first time Darius said, "We had a good talk the other day. Maybe she is ready to stay with me for a little while."

"Darius, I don't think that is a good idea. You guys only been talking for a few days. You hurt her deeply." Alexis said passionately.

"I know, Lexie. The best way to work through this is to spend more time together. I'm not going to force anything on her. She could even stay in the spare bedroom. I just don't want her to be alone right now."

"Jus, I don't want her to feel like she isn't welcome at our home."

"She knows better than that, Lex. I just want us to spend the night together without any distractions." Justin explained.

"Do you think Rick has some news for us, Jus?" Darius asked.

"I'm sure he has something, or he wouldn't have asked for the meeting. Anyway, that's all for now. I have a few meetings to attend to. I will see both of you later tonight."

"Jus, thank you, man for taking care of this. I hope we don't have to worry about Sky. I just want to try to mend my relationship with Ciara and throw myself into this new position I haven't been able to enjoy." Darius said.

"We will be ready for whatever comes our way. Lex could you stay for a minute?" Justin asked his wife.

"Sure." Alexis responded as they watched Darius leave the room.

"I love you. Thanks, from the bottom of my heart for giving DK another chance. It bothered me to no end to know you guys were at each other throats."

"I love you too, Jus. I know deep down Darius is a good man."

Justin and Alexis talked for a few minutes longer until she told him she had to get to a meeting.

Chapter Fourteen

Darius went to his office after his meeting with Justin and Alexis. For the first time since they had broken up, he felt that he and Ciara had a chance to mend their relationship. He was so nervous the other night when they arrived at Justin's house. He couldn't believe that Ciara was more beautiful then he remembered. They made small talk for about ten minutes when Justin told them that they could meet privately in his home office. Once they were seated he waited for Ciara to begin.

Ciara sat in the big chair behind Justin's desk while Darius sat in the center chair in front of the desk. "Darius it's hard to know where to start."

"Take your time, Ciara. There is no need for you to rush anything." Darius responded.

"I've had a lot of time to think about all that has happened between us lately." Ciara took a deep breath then continued. "I need for you to open up to me about what happened to you in Florida."

Darius was nervous to talk about his time in Florida. Outside of spending time with his parents the trip was a total disaster. "Where would you like for me to start?"

"You can start by telling me your marital status."

"Ciara, I'm not married, nor have I ever been married." I understand why you're concerned about this, but it's not true."

"Why is it so hard for you to be upfront with all of us about what went on in Florida? Justin and Lexie should have been told right away about all of this before it gotten to this level."

"I just wanted to leave that part of my life behind me. The only good thing that came out of living there was spending time with my parents before they passed away."

"I know it may be painful, but we could have avoided a lot of what's going on right now if you had been straight with all of us."

The Candidate: Back to Business

"I know that now, but at the time a fresh start was what I thought was best for all of us. My head was totally messed up when I left Michigan. I thought being in a different environment would help me to work out the demons I've been fighting for most of my adult life."

"What made you go into therapy, Darius?" Ciara asked.

"I found myself totally depressed when I wasn't looking after my parents. I knew I needed to heal physically and emotionally after everything that happened at the press conference."

"I still don't know how you and Justin could handle all that madness. When Lexie told me about all that you guys went through I felt the pain."

"I told my mom before she passed away that I needed to figure out why I always picked the wrong woman, especially women outside of my race."

"Were you able to figure that out, Darius?" Ciara asked with an anxious look on her face.

"Not totally. When I first started therapy I thought I was making progress. Deep down I guess I was looking for someone that was passive, so I didn't have to put too much into a relationship."

Ciara's sudden laugh startled Darius. "From what I heard you definitely picked the wrong woman when you hooked up with Roslyn."

"I know. She played me from start to finish. I cared for her a lot, but I was broken up when I finally realized she just wanted me so she could beat Jus out of the CEO seat."

"I'm so glad you guys didn't let that relationship destroy your friendship."

"We almost did. I couldn't believe some of the things I did to my best friend all for a seat I knew I had no chance in hell of winning."

"Okay. Let's get back to Florida, Darius. Was your therapist able to help you to figure out the choices you made when it came to women?"

"Well, she got the ball rolling. I had to dig deep down into my inner self. That is when I realized it wasn't the women I picked that caused me so many problems, but it was me. For some unknown reason I felt that I didn't deserve a good woman."

"Why is that Darius?"

"When I looked at my parents, Jus' parents, and even Lexie's parents, I used to see boring instead of something special. Hell, even Jus and Lexie's marriage at times I used to look at as boring, even though Lexie kept Jus on his toes."

"I need to ask you a question. Please be honest. Are you afraid of commitment?"

Darius thought for a moment before he answered. "I was until after my parents died. It took them passing away for me to realize the relationship they had is what I truly want."

"What do you want from me, Darius?"

"Happily, every after. I want what all the people I mention have. I know there will be ups and downs, but I know I have grown enough to stick it out when the downs come into play."

With tears rolling down her face Ciara said, "I want that too, Darius. I'm still afraid of opening myself up to you again, but I miss you so much. Getting my relationship back on track with Lexie helped me tremendously, but I need us to start again. This time we need to take it slow."

Darius couldn't believe what he just heard. "We can take it as slow as you like, Ciara. I want to prove to you that I am the right man for you and that I will do whatever it takes to make our relationship work."

"That's good to hear, Darius. I'm glad you understand. I'm going to stay with my sister for a little while. Lexie and Justin need their space."

"What wrong with coming to my place? You can stay in the spare bedroom."

The Candidate: Back to Business

"We're not ready to be that close again, Darius."

"I know you're right. How about we start with having dinner?"

"That's cool. Now, I think we better get back in there so we can give the lovebirds some quiet time." Ciara and Darius stayed a few hours longer before they left and went their separate ways.

Darius came back to the present. He finally felt he had something to look forward to. He was going to do everything in his power to win back Ciara's trust and love. He was so hyped about this he was going to ask Justin to give some pointers. He was so proud of his best friend. Alexis took him thru hell and back when they first started their relationship, Justin hung in there. There were many times when Darius tried to get Justin to break up with Alexis. There were many females friends of theirs that would have loved to take Alexis' place, but Justin only had eyes for Alexis from the first day they met. Knowing it was time to get back to work Darius pushed those thoughts to the back of his mind.

Chapter Fifteen

The next day Darius sat with a big smile on his face. He couldn't wait for him and Ciara to go out to dinner over the weekend. He knew he had to be patient but all he could think about was getting their relationship back on track. She was one special lady and this time he was going to make sure nothing came between them. With that thought on his mind he was motivated to move full force into this Skylar thing. He had to get that crazy woman out of his life once and for all. He dreaded that he had to take precious time to deal with this situation, but it will be well worth it.

Darius was brought out of his daydreams when he heard someone banging on his front door. He left the kitchen heading to see who was so anxious to see him. He pulled the door open without checking to see who was on the other side. Seeing Ciara on the other side of the door made his heart skip a beat until he saw the angry look on her pretty face.

"Baby what's wrong?" Darius asked with concerned.

Ciara pushed her way into Darius' condo. When she reached the living room she sat on the sofa. "You got to do something. I can't take this any longer." Ciara said with tears in her voice.

"What happened, Ciara?"

"My sister and I went to my place so I could pick up some of my things. We walked into what looked like a war zone. Every room was tossed and most of my business clothes were tossed in the bathtub full of water."

Darius couldn't believe what he was hearing. "I'm sorry baby. Let's think about this. It could be just a random break in. I can get why you would think that it is Sky."

"I don't want to hear that, Darius. You know this is the work of that crazy heifer. I'm going to the police station to file a report. We just left without touching anything. My sister had to go to work. I had no intention of staying there by myself."

"Let's head to your place and call the police on the way over. Don't worry baby. We will get to the bottom of this." Darius and Ciara left his condo then headed over to Ciara's.

The police pulled up behind Darius and Ciara as soon as they arrived back at Ciara's house. Rick and another plain clothed detective exit the vehicle. The chief introduced Detective Fred Sims and told them to wait outside while they go in to make sure no one was still on the premises. Darius and Ciara entered her house once Detective Sims said that it was okay for them to go in.

"I want that woman picked up right now and put behind bars where she belongs." Ciara said angrily.

"Calm down baby." Darius said quietly.

"Don't tell me to calm down. Look at my house. How did that psychopath get in here?"

"It seems that someone came through a broken basement window." Rick replied."

"I can't believe this. I'm never going to have any peace." Ciara said pacing around her living room floor.

"So, I guess I don't have to guess at who you feel is behind this Ms. Gleason?"

"No, you don't. This is that woman doing a poor job of staking her claim."

"Ciara, maybe we should keep an open mind. This could be a coincident."

"Yeah right." Ciara said sarcastically.

"So, you may know who would do this to you Ms. Gleason?" Detective Sims asked.

"Yes, Darius' crazy ex that followed him here from Florida." Ciara responded.

"Can you take a look around to see if anything is missing, Ms. Gleason." The chief asked.

Ciara walked around her home with Darius following behind her. Returning back into the living room she said, "No, I can't see that anything was taken, but that fool just made a mess of everything."

"What do we need to do next, Rick?" Darius asked.

"I will file this report, but I would need concrete proof that this is the handiwork of Dr. Stevens." Rick said.

"I've lived in this house for almost ten years without so much as an unwanted guest, but now it's totally disheveled. That is not a coincidence.

"Be that as it may we can't go around arresting people without having evidence that they committed a crime." Detective Sims chimed in.

"Well, if you excuse me, I will go savage whatever I can from all this mess." Ciara walked angrily out of the living room.

"You can understand why she is upset. We have to find Skylar. I agree with Ciara. This has her written all over this." Darius said.

"We'll leave you guys to this. I will put extra patrol into finding Dr. Stevens." Rick took down a few other notes then they took their leave.

The Candidate: Back to Business

Chapter Sixteen

Justin was sitting at his desk going over the notes he jotted down for the next board meeting. It had been a long morning. It was nearly one o'clock and time for him to take a break for lunch. He wished Alexis was free, but she had a few outside meetings to attend, then she was headed home. He didn't know if Darius was at work since he been so busy. He decided after he finished his notes he would check to see if Darius was at work and see if he was available to get a bite to eat. With that thought on his mind the person he was just thinking about knocked on his door and walked in then sat in one of the two chairs that was in front of Justin's desk.

"Wow, I was just thinking about hitting you up to see if you are available for lunch." Justin said.

"Sure, I could use a drink right about now."

A worried look came across Justin's face, "Isn't it a little early for a drink?"

"Not after the morning I've had. Ciara came over this morning banging on my door. Someone trashed her home. After the police left we grab a few a Ciara's things then went to hire a private investigator."

"Why didn't you call me and let me know what was going on?"

"Everything happened so fast. I decided to fill you in once I got here."

"Lex is going to have a fit. She is going to insist Ciara comes back to stay with us until Skylar is found."

"Good luck with that one. She is determined to leave her sister's and go back home. I'm supposed to meet her there later to help her clean up."

"I'm going to wait before I fill Lex in on what's going on. I know she would want to help you guys get the house back in order. Let's get out of here. I need a drink too."

Later that evening Justin, Alexis, Darius, and Ciara took a break once they put Ciara's house back in order. Ciara explained that her sister was upset with her because she decided to stay home. Ciara was upset with herself because she forgot to put her security system on the last time she left so the she nor police weren't notified about the break in. Alexis was on the same page with her sister. She didn't want Ciara to stay at her house. Then they all tried to get her to let Darius stay with her, but she didn't like that idea neither.

"Ciara, you are making us crazy. We all live too far to get to you if you have an emergency." Alexis said frustrated that her friend wouldn't let any of them help her.

"I need to get back to normal. I'm not going to let that crazy heifer have me to be scared to stay in my own home." Ciara insisted.

"Baby, we are just worried about you. I will stay on the PI, but it may take a while before he could find out where Sky is hiding out." Darius added.

Hearing Skylar's name made Ciara angrier then she was when she arrived home to find her home had been ransacked. "I'm not going to hide out and let that woman control my life. I will be extra careful, but I refuse to turn my life upside down."

Before anyone could say anything else Darius cell phone rang. "Hello this is Darius."

"Darius, this is Phil. Wanted to give you an update. I am sitting across the street from where the subject is living."

Darius was amazed. The police hadn't come up with anything in days, but Phil was able to locate Skylar within hours. "This is great news. Where are you? I want to meet you there."

"That's not a good ideal. I will give you a report first thing in the morning. I think you will be amazed."

"I want to call the police. She has to be questioned." Darius insisted.

"We can take care of that in the morning. I will not let her out of my site."

"I don't understand why you want me to wait. She needs to be locked up."

"You need to give me time to gather evidence. There isn't anything the police can do if you don't have concrete proof that she is behind everything that has been going on."

"Okay. Meet me at my office at eight in the morning. I'm going to have Ciara and my business associates in on the meeting since this is affecting their lives."

"Will do. See you in the morning, Darius. I will have a few of my men staking out the subject while I'm meeting with you."

"That was Phil the private investigator I hired. He has found Sky."

"We heard your side of the conversation that nut case needs to be picked up now." Ciara said.

"Baby, Phil was right. We need concrete evidence that Sky is guilty. He is anxious to share what he has found out so far."

"Ciara, since we all have to meet in the morning please come home with me or go home with Darius. Better yet let him stay in your guest bedroom. I won't be able to sleep tonight knowing that you are alone." Alexis begged.

"Fine. Darius, you can stay just for tonight."

"Cool. Thank you baby. We appreciate you changing your mind.

Chapter Seventeen

Justin, Alexis, Darius, and Ciara arrived at the office the next morning an hour before they were to meet with Phillip Powers. As they waited in the small conference room, they seemed to be in their own thoughts. Justin didn't like the fact that Alexis tossed and turned most of the previous night. He knew she was worried about Ciara. Looking at the faces that were filled with concern, Justin decided to break the ice.

"Would anyone like something to drink or eat before we get started?"

"Nothing for me, babe. I can't digest anything right now." Alexis responded to her husband.

"Me either. I have a full day ahead once we're done here." Ciara said a little distracted.

"Jus, I will go down to the café to get us some coffee and bagels" Darius said right before leaving the room.

"He is nervous about the meeting this morning." Ciara said.

"To be honest so am I." Justin added.

"Jus, why do you think Rick wasn't able to find out anything on Skylar?" Alexis was curious since Phillip was able to pick up her trail right away.

"The police department has different procedures to follow then the private investigators (PI). PI's are able to move around more freely and Rick said he was short staffed."

"Well, I just hope all of this ends soon and peacefully." Ciara stated just as Darius walked back into the room with refreshments. Fifteen minutes later Phillip was shown into the conference room by Sage. They decided to meet there instead of Darius' office.

"Good morning everyone." Phillip said with a big smile on his face.

The Candidate: Back to Business

"That depends on what you about to share with us. This is Justin and Alexis. Of course, you remember meeting Ciara. Everyone this is Phillip Powers the PI I hired" Darius spoke in a professional tone.

"Glad to meet you all. I would like to start off with where Dr. Stevens has been hanging out. As a matter of fact, she has been only a few blocks away from you, Darius.

"You've got to be kidding."

"No, I'm serious. What is interesting is that she's not there as often as the person she's been visiting wants her to be. This is according to the conversation I've overheard." Phillip explained.

"If she's not there that often do you know where she spends her time outside of harassing us? Darius asked full of concerned.

"Let me try to break it down before I go further. The reason I found Dr. Stevens so quickly is because I've been investigating the person she's been visiting for the last three months."

"We were wondering how you found out her location so quickly when the police have been working on her whereabouts much longer." Ciara commented.

"This is where the business aspect comes in. I can't divulge too much information, but Dr. Stevens has been visiting Harrison Harper." Taking a deep breath after noticing the shock looks on their faces Phillip continued. "Darius when you told me about the business dynamics of WES this became all too familiar."

"I'm not following. How does Harrison fit into all of this? I know he wasn't happy when he left the company, but he didn't seem angry." Justin asked.

"I've done a lot of work following up on angry ex-employees. When Darius told me about the competition for the CEO seat and later your inherited the company, Justin (if I may call you that) that didn't sit well with me. We have both of you with people that are mad at you all"

Darius took a long look at Phillip. "Okay. Don't leave us in suspense. Tell us what you have uncovered?"

"Well, I didn't want to stop there. The next point of contention is running a check on Shane Gibbons, Tucker Westbrook, and Kristen Carson. It's too early in the investigation to speculate." Taking a quick breath, Phillip continued. "Harrison Harper is a different story. I don't have it locked down how long they've communicating, but he and Dr. Stevens are mighty chumming." Phillip explained.

"Oh my God. I should have known Harrison wasn't going to walk away from WES quietly." Justin said mad at himself for not suspecting Harrison's involvement. Now he knows why he left with too much fuss.

"How in the world would Skylar know Harrison?" Alexis asked.

Before Phillip could answer Alexis' question, Justin said. "Hold on a minute. I don't think that is necessary to check out my staff. We thoroughly investigate all our employees. I know there were some hurt feelings when DK was promoted over these individuals, but I had a long one-on-one talk with each of these employees. They are not involved." Justin said not liking Phillip interference in his company.

"With all due respect, Justin; I just want to widen my investigation. You will be surprised at how many companies fail because of disgruntled present and past employees." Phillip continued.

Darius put his head down. He was upset with himself for telling so much of his life to Skylar. "I'm sure Harrison came up in my sessions, Lexie." Darius answered Alexis' earlier question.

Phillip added. "Dr. Stevens arrived at his home around six o'clock last night. She hadn't left by the time my backup came at five o'clock this morning. He reported she didn't leave until six thirty. He is trailing her and will provide an update in a few hours."

"We have big trouble on our hands with Harrison bitterness towards WES and Justin and Sky's obsession with me. This is getting out of hand." Darius said mostly thinking out loud.

The Candidate: Back to Business

Wrapping it up, Phillip said, "That is all I have for now. I will keep you posted as soon as I get additional details." Phillip stood then headed out the door after shaking everyone's hands.

"I'll talk to you guys later. I need to get to work." Ciara said leaving out behind Phillip.

"We better get to work too." Alexis said as she gave Justin a slight kiss on his cheek then Justin and Darius pounded their fists before leaving.

Justin headed to his office. Once there he sat in his chair. He had to think what to do about Harrison. Knowing Harrison and Skylar were conspiring against them didn't sit well at all. One was an egomaniac while the other was a psychopath. He felt a huge weigh on his shoulders to protect his family and employees.

Thinking back to the old days, Harrison used to be a valuable part of WES, but once the race for the CEO seat was underway he changed. Harrison thought with his father relationship with Ross, he was a shoo-in for the CEO seat. Harrison had started to change towards the end of the competition. He became destructive. That was during Ross' last days at WES when his health started to deteriorate. When Justin inherited WES, he quickly found out all the petty things Harrison were doing including gossiping, withholding information, and interfering with other employees projects.

In the end Justin was glad that Harrison quit before he had to fire him. He had been thinking about creating something special for Harrison to take over, but after finding out his negative behaviors he put a hold on that project. Knowing that it was time for him to get back to work, Justin put that and the morning events behind him and concentrated on dealing with his workday.

Chapter Eighteen

Later that afternoon Justin received a call from Rick requesting a meeting with him. He was glad to hear from the police department. Hopefully he had more positive information to report since what they receive from Phillip wasn't good. After he meet with Rick, Justin knew he couldn't put off meeting with Harrison any longer. He thought about taking Darius with him but thought it would be better to meet with Harrison alone. He wasn't going to even tell Alexis because she would try to talk him out of it. He was at a lost about what to do but doing nothing wasn't an option. Before he could continue with that thought Sage showed Rick into his office.

"Good afternoon, Rick. How is the investigation going?" Justin didn't have time for small talk.

"It's coming along. I have some interesting news to share with you." Rick replied.

"I'm all ears."

"It seems that Dr. Stevens arrived here two weeks after Darius' return. She only stayed for a few days then about a month later she moved here permanently. The kicker is that the house she's living in is only a few blocks away from Darius'."

"What has she been doing all this time?" Justin asked.

"From the information I gathered she's been laying low, but she also has been doing research on you and your company." Rick explained.

That news didn't sit well with Justin at all. "Why is she so interested in me and WES?"

"Well, it seems that she has an accomplice working with her. This lady has been very busy."

This information threw Justin for a loop. He thought Rick was talking about Harrison when he mentioned an accomplice. "What have they been doing all this time?"

The Candidate: Back to Business

"The deed to the house is registered in her housemate's name, Danae Davenport. She's thirty-two years old and her occupation is designer. She also happens to be Dr. Stevens' stepsister"

"We will be bringing Ms. Davenport in for questioning. We found out that she has been the one making those harassing calls to Ciara."

"What about the newspaper leak and the break-in at Ciara's house?"

"Sorry, so far we have not been able to link neither of them with those incidents."

"Have you come up with anything else, Rick?" Justin was curious if the police had found out about Harrison's involvement.

"Yes. There's also a connection between Dr. Stevens and Harrison Harper." Rick stops and takes a closer look at Justin. "By the expression on your face this isn't news to you."

"I recently received this information. As a matter of fact I was going to pay Harrison a visit when I leave here today."

"I don't know if that is a good idea, Justin."

"Why not?"

"I'm aware of the past issues between you and Harrison. People are still talking about that press conference years later. I know there is bad blood so a visit may not be wise."

"I need to do something to find out what they are up to. It was bad enough that we must deal with Harrison and Skylar, but now you're telling me that there is a third person involved."

"I'm not getting any good vibes with this, Justin. Hold on tight. Give me a few days to see what else I can come up with before you pay Harrison a visit. We don't know the state of mind of him or his cohorts."

"I hear what you're saying, Rick, but I feel helpless at times. I have to protect my family and employees."

"I promise you we're working hard to get this resolved. I have to go for now. I will let you know how the interview went with Ms. Davenport."

"I'll sit tight for the time being. Let me walk out with you. Lex will be happy that I'm home early for a change." Justin headed home to give Alexis an update on the case.

When Justin arrived home he wasn't surprised to see Darius and Ciara's cars in his driveway. Alexis probably couldn't get off the phone fast enough to have them to come over. Justin didn't mind because he didn't feel up to repeating the conversation he had with Rick twice. As soon as he walked in the door the twins rushed him telling him how they beat the pants off their friends in basketball. It's not the career he wanted for his sons, but he may have to accept that they're not going into the family business. Justin looked around the living for a few seconds then was heading towards the family room where Allie came running out of nearly knocking him over. He didn't know where his daughter got the energy.

"Hey, Lil Bit. How's it going?"

"Me a big girl now." Allie responded.

"It's I not me, Allie." Jeremy corrected his baby sister.

With a mean look on her face, Allie said. "Me is better."

"That's enough kids. Boys take your sister, and you all get washed up for dinner." Alexis said.

"No. Me is clean." Allie protested.

"Listen to your mom, Allie." Justin said and a stern voice.

"Alright." Allie stomped all the way up the stairs with the twins following close behind her.

The Candidate: Back to Business

"You guys are going to catch it with that one. She is too much like both of you." Darius said with a smirk on his face.

"I second that. We all going to have to gear up to keep that one under control." Ciara added.

"Whatever. She knows not to go too far, or I will snatch her up. What do you have to tell us, Jus?" Alexis asked.

"We can talk after we put the kids to bed. Right now all I want to do is take a quick shower and eat." Justin replied.

"Okay. Ciara you and Darius can help me set the table so we can get ready to eat when Jus and the kids are ready."

"Sure. Nothing I like better then working with two beautiful women. Even if one of them is being bossy."

"Stop complaining, Darius. You need to earn your keep. We all know by the time you are done there won't be any leftovers." Ciara teased.

The trio worked swiftly getting everything ready. By the time Justin and the kids came down the room was quite because all you could hear was everyone in the room enjoying their dinner.

Chapter Nineteen

The looks on every face after Justin told them about his conversation with Rick was unbelievable. They keep interrupting him with questions. Justin even told them about his intentions on visiting Rick without letting them know. He knew there was going to be hell to pay from Alexis tonight for letting that thought cross his mind. She told him all three individuals involved in the case were loose cannons and that no one should attempt a meeting with any of them alone. The room was silent for a few minutes, so Justin broke the ice.

"Listen everyone. I think Rick is right. We need to lay low and let the police and Phil handle things."

"I think the least we should do is go down to the police station to see if they're going to lock that psycho up that has been making those harassing phone calls to me." Ciara said.

"No. Rick will get back to us on that. What we can do is see if Phil can try to figure out their next move. With the press moving on they have to be planning something else just as disruptive." Justin stated.

"You're right, Jus. We need to be prepared. I'll give Phil a call." Darius said leaving the room.

"I don't like this, Jus. What is it going to take to get those crazy fools to leave us alone?"

"When I get to the office in the morning I'm going to use my contacts to see what Harrison have been doing in the business world. He is a workaholic, so I know he has to be working somewhere since he left WES."

"I wish Darius hurry up with his call. I need to head home. I have a busy day planned tomorrow." Ciara said.

"You are going to let Darius go home with you, Ciara?"

"There hasn't been any trouble since the break-in, so I don't feel it's necessary for him to be camping out with me."

Don't start that, Ciara. You know we had an agreement." Alexis said.

"I don't need a babysitter, Lexie." Ciara said not willing to give in this time to her best friend.

"Lex is right, Ciara. We all have to be careful. These fools have something planned and until we know what we…" Justin didn't get a chance to finish his statement because Darius came back into the room.

"I think it's going down. Phil said the police went by the house that Sky and Danae is living, and they had to call for backup because Danae didn't want to go in quietly."

"Were they able to take her in?" Ciara asked.

"Yes. The good news is they had to take Sky in also. She interfered and didn't want them to take Danae."

"This is great news. Now you can stop worrying, Lexie. I don't need Darius to stay with me tonight." Ciara was happy to hear that both Skylar and Danae were picked up.

"Ciara, we still need to be careful. What if they are not able to detain them? I'll feel much better if Darius is there with you. Even if it's only for tonight."

"I need my space, Darius. I wish you all would understand that."

"We do, Ciara. The decision is yours." Alexis said. She was sick of trying to talk sense into Ciara. All she could do now is pray for her friend.

"Good. I'm going home now. Darius, I really appreciated you staying with me, but I don't feel it's necessary any longer." Ciara gave all of them a brief hug and left.

"Why do she have to be so stubborn? We're just trying to protect her." Darius said. He felt defeated.

"We just have to pray all will be well for her since the police picked Skylar and Danae up." Justin tried to reassure his best friend.

"I know what I can do. I'll see if Rick can post someone at her place. If not I will sit there. She doesn't have to know."

"Darius, I don't think that is a good idea. You guys have been getting along well since all of this happened. You don't want to make her angry again." Alexis said cautiously.

"I know. I just want her to be safe. I have bad dreams about what if she was home during the break-in. I wouldn't be able to live with myself if something happened to her."

"DK just stay here or go home. Ciara will be alright. We have a busy day tomorrow wrapping up the loose ends from the press conference."

"Okay. I just can't wait until this is over. I do need to head home and fix up my place a little before I turn in. The place is a mess since I just rush in to grab the things I will need while I was over Ciara's.

"I'm sure Rick and Phil should have more news for us in the morning. I'll walk you out." Justin and Darius left the room. Alexis stayed in the family room where they met. She had an uneasy feeling about what is going to happen next. She knew she was smothering Ciara and that she needed to stop before she pushes her away again. She doesn't know if she should run this by Justin or not. He had the right idea that someone needed to approach Harrison. The situation wasn't good, but she always had a good professional relationship with Harrison. Maybe she should be the one to find out what he's been up to. Seeing that as a possible solution it was time for her to turn in. She had to be well rested to deal with Harrison.

The Candidate: Back to Business

Chapter Twenty

The next morning Justin, Alexis, and Darius had a brief meeting. They hadn't heard anything from the police or Phil, so they decided to work and let the authorities do their thing. Justin and Darius had to work on the finishing touches for the statement that Darius will post for the media. Alexis told them she had a few outside appointments and would see Justin at home later that evening. Both men were distracted so they didn't give Alexis their full attention or else they would have notice how nervous she was acting. Leaving the men to their work Alexis stopped by her office picked up a few of the designs she had been working on and left the office.

Alexis pulled up in front of the huge house where Harrison resided. She took a look around to make sure Phil didn't have any of his staff staking out Harrison's house. She knew this may not be a good idea, but she had to do something to help out her family and best friend. She has always been persuasive, so she felt she would be able to get Harrison to slip and let them know what their next move would be. Taking a deep breath Alexis headed for Harrison's front door. Again she looked around and didn't see no one in site. Ringing the doorbell a couple of times and waiting for an answer Alexis jumped with Harrison pulled open the door abruptly.

"What the hell are you doing here?" A disheveled Harrison asked.

Alexis couldn't believe her eyes. The man standing on the other side of the door looked nothing like the well-kept handsome man that used to work at WES.

"Good morning to you too, Harrison." Alexis said ignoring Harrison's bad mood as she walked into the house.

"What's so good about it?"

"How about you woke up this morning."

"It's too early in the morning to hear that garbage."

"You look like hell, Harrison. What's going on with you?"

"What do you mean? Getting forced out a company that was should have been yours isn't enough to make you go mad?"

"We didn't force you out, Harrison you quit. Justin was searching for a way to create a new position for you that would elevate your career."

"Yeah right. I believe in the Easter bunny too."

"Why are you so negative? With your experience we could have taken WES to the next level."

"I put my heart and soul in that company. Ross owed it to my dad to give me that promotion and the company."

"Justin earned that promotion fair and square. As for inheriting the company that was the furthest from our minds. We had no idea Ross was planning on leaving the company to Justin."

"You can leave now. I don't believe a word that's coming out of your mouth."

"What have you been doing, Harrison? Is there anything I can do to help?"

"Sure is. Get the hell out of my house. Make sure you don't come back."

"I'm sorry you feel that way, Harrison. All I wanted to do was see if I could be of help to you. Please take care of yourself."

Out of nowhere Harrison turned red and charged towards Alexis. Once he was standing in front of her he started yelling incoherently. "I told you to get out." Harrison put his hands around Alexis' neck. Alexis started fighting for her life. She was able to knee Harrison in the groin. Since Harrison was so drunk he stumble backwards a little bit while still holding onto Alexis' neck. Alexis was able to break free then headed towards the front door. All she could remember after that was everything went black.

Justin and Darius were sitting in Justin's home office. Justin was worried because Alexis hadn't arrived home yet. She hadn't even call to check in on the kids. Justin called her mom, Ciara, and a few of Alexis's other friends. He even called her assistant to check and see where Alexis' outside appointments were. He became even more tense when she told him that Alexis didn't have any outside appointments on her calendar. Justin was quiet for a few minutes after making the calls, so Darius decided to break the silence.

"Jus, I'm sure Lexie will be home soon."

"Something is wrong, DK. Lex would never be out like this without reaching out to someone."

"Let me call Ciara again… Darius didn't get the chance to finish his statement because his phone rang. It was Phil.

"What's up, Phil?"

"Just checking in. Things have been quiet since the ladies have been picked up. I'm still having my people to stakeout Harrison and Dr. Stevens' residences.

"Has there been anything exciting going on at Harrison's place?"

"He's been barricaded in his house for the last few days. According to my contact he's only had one visitor. She's been there for a while now."

"I sure hope it's not someone else that is part of their destructive plan?"

"According to my guy she was too sophisticated to be mixed up with the likes of these fools."

"Okay. If that's it I have a call to make." Darius stated trying to end their conversation.

"That's it for now. I'll keep you posted."

"Cool thanks, Phil." Darius ended the call then punched in number one to call Ciara. Her voice mail picked up, so he left a message.

Hey babe. Just checking in. I forgot about your nail appointment. I was hoping Lexie was with you or that you heard from her. Call me when you get a chance. Love you. After leaving the message, Darius returned his attention back to Justin. "Sorry man I forgot Ciara had a nail appointment. I'm sure she will call me back once she is done."

"I just wish Lex, or someone will call me to let me know she is okay."

"While we're waiting on a call back how about a pool rematch? I owe you a beat down." Darius suggested.

"Whatever. I guess we can pass the time. It's driving me crazy just sitting here worrying about Lex." Justin and Darius headed down to his man cave. On his way downstairs Justin couldn't shake the feeling that something bad had happened to Alexis.

The Candidate: Back to Business

Chapter Twenty-One

Justin and Darius were seated again in Justin's home office. Darius couldn't believe even while being distracted with Alexis' disappearance that Justin still beat him two out of the three games they played. He was so worried about his best friend. Justin hasn't been this out of it since he and Alexis was on the outs when she told him she was pregnant with Allyson. Justin was preoccupied with some papers that sat in front of him on his desk. Every so often Justin would glance up from the papers to look at the picture on his desk of him and Alexis on their wedding day. The silence was driving Darius crazy, so he decided to start a conversation that may take his mind off his worries for a bit.

"Jus, do you think I have a real shot at getting Ciara back?"

Shaking his head a little trying to get his mind off worrying about Alexis, Justin said, "Yes I do. She seems to be more open about getting back with you and Lex said that she is getting back to feeling comfortable around you again."

"I sure hope so. I love that girl so much. I didn't think I could love anyone more than I loved Roslyn. I know our relationship was toxic, but Roslyn was the first relationship I put my all into."

"I know you don't have to tell me. I lived it remember."

"Yes I do remember. I have so many regrets about the things I done during that time. I just want to… Darius didn't finish his statement because his phone rang, and it was Ciara. He was so happy to see her face pop up on his screen.

"Hi babe. Thanks for calling me back."

"No problem. I was going to call as soon as I was done anyways to see if you guys heard from Lexie yet?"

"No we haven't. I'm here with Jus now so I'm going to put you on speaker phone."

"Hey, Ciara. I don't mean to be rude, but have you heard from Lex?" Justin asked his wife's best friend.

"No I haven't heard from her since this morning. She told me she had a few outside errands to run. She said you guys had just finished your meeting." Ciara responded.

"Did she sound worried or distracted?" Justin continued to question Ciara.

"No she actually sounded kind of excited. I'm sorry I can't be of more help. Do you need me to come over?"

"No that isn't necessary. I'll let you finish your conversation with DK. I'm going to try Lex's mom again." Justin left the room.

"Hey babe. I'm so worried about Jus. I haven't seen him this distracted in a long time."

I'm kind of concerned too. Lexie doesn't go missing in action like this. She is still leery about leaving Allie for too long." Ciara said trying to figure out why Alexis hasn't gotten in touch with anyone.

"I'll let you go for now. I hear Jus returning. I know he isn't going to just sit around and wait. I'll keep you posted."

"Okay. Thanks, Darius."

"No problem babe. Love you." Darius was a little disappointment when Ciara didn't say she loved him back before they got off the phone. Putting that thought aside, Darius wasn't surprised to hear Justin next words.

"I'm not going to just sit around waiting when I could be out there looking for my wife."

"You wouldn't have any place to start, Jus."

"Sure I do. I'm going down to the police station to file a missing person's report."

"It's too soon to file a missing person's report, Jus."

"No it's not. You can file a report earlier than the standard forty-eight to seventy-two hours if there is suspected foul play."

"The ladies have been picked up. Lexie isn't in any danger, Jus."

"I'm not taking any chances. I'm headed to see Rick right now. He better have some addition news about what these crazy fools are up to. Are you coming?" Justin saw Darius shake his head yes then they both headed out to the police station.

Alexis was slowly regaining consciousness. She couldn't figure out where she was at first. All she knew was her head was hurting and she couldn't move her arms or legs. Moving her head again she realized her mouth was bound too. The room she was in was semi dark. Looking around it appeared to be a bedroom. There was a queen size bed with two night stands on either side. On the other side of the room there was a long dresser with a mirror attached, with a computer desk on the side of the room with a desktop computer, printer, and a small lamp. After looking around her surroundings, Alexis tried to remember what happened to her and where she was being held. Then her argument with Harrison came flooding back to her. A few minutes later Harrison entered the room. Alexis was surprised that he had showered and dressed. He looked more like the Harrison she was used to seeing.

"Sleeping beauty decides to wake up." Harrison said in an uninteresting voice.

Alexis couldn't speak since her mouth was taped, but she looked at Harrison with the evil eye.

"Don't be cutting your eyes at me" Harrison said angrily then turned on the light as he walked further into the room. "I'm going to take the tape off your mouth. If you scream you're going to regret the day you were born. Do I make myself clear?" Harrison and Alexis stared each other down and he didn't attempt to take the tape off her mouth until she nodded that she wouldn't scream. Instead of taking the tape off in one movement, Harrison slowly removed the tape enjoying the pain he caused Alexis. Once the tape was off Harrison didn't say anything for about thirty seconds to be sure Alexis was going to keep her promise.

"Now you want to follow the rules. You should have gotten out of my house the first time I told you, but no you had to run off at the mouth."

Clearing her throat, Alexis said, "What is wrong with you, Harrison? Why are you doing this to me?"

"It's starting already. I guess you want to play the victim?"

"I want to go home, Harrison."

"I want my company back. I guess neither of us are going to get what we want." Harrison said with a crazy laugh.

"This is not going to work. I know people are out there looking for me."

"So. They could look all they want. They won't find you here. I removed all traces of you."

Alexis didn't like the sound of that. She now wished she had listened to Justin and not come over here to confront this fool. "What are you going to do to me? You can't keep me locked up forever."

"I don't need forever. Don't try to get any details out of me. Unfortunately, you will have to suffer. I'm not going to be able to free you to relieve yourself. You have already proven you can't be trusted. I have to leave now." Before Harrison left the room he went over to the dresser where he left the roll of duct tape then put tape back on Alexis' mouth. Without another word he turned then left the room.

The Candidate: Back to Business

Chapter Twenty-Two

Justin and Darius sat in the lobby at the police station waiting on Rick to come out to talk to them. Justin was quiet on the way over to the station. He didn't feel like talking. He ignored Darius small talk. After a while Darius got the hint and he was quiet the rest of the ride. Once they were in the police station and asked to see Rick the officer at the front desk told them to have a seat while he sees if the Chief was available. They had been there about fifteen minutes when Darius' phone rang.

"Hey, Phil what's up?"

"Just wanted to call with an update. Dr. Steven's has been released. My guy told me she arrived at Harrison's house about a half hour ago."

"You can't be serious."

"Sorry, I am. She didn't look happy."

"What about his other visitor? Is she still there?"

"No, she left hours ago. There hadn't been any other activity outside of Dr. Stevens's arrival."

"Okay keep me posted." Darius ended his call with Phil then turned to look at Justin.

"Don't tell me I heard you correctly. Skylar isn't in custody."

"No she's not. She is at Harrison's house right now."

"I can't believe this." Justin stood from his chair and rushed over to the counter to talk to the office. He was yelling and at one point attempted to collar the officer. Darius grabbed Justin to try to calm him down but that didn't stop several officers from coming to the aid of their fellow officer at the front desk. At the moment where things were getting out of control Rick showed up. He told the officers to back down and he will take care of the situation. Rick ushered Justin and Darius into his office.

"Are you insane man? Why were you cutting up out there? You could have gotten yourself killed."

"Why the hell is Skylar out walking the streets?" Justin asked angrily.

"I was finishing up here then I was going to stop by your house to let you know we didn't have enough evidence to hold her."

"Why the hell not?" Justin continued.

"She was only brought in because she was giving us problems when we picked up her step-sister."

Darius spoke for the first time. "So this Danae is still in custody?"

"Yes. She has some outstanding warrants in Florida so she will be extradited back there."

"So, nothing is going to be done about her harassing Ciara?"

"Not at the moment. The charges she's facing in Florida could land her in prison for years."

Justin didn't care about any of that. "I need to put in a missing person's report."

"Really. On whom?" Rick asked.

"Lex has been missing since this morning."

"That isn't long enough to put in a report, Justin." Rick explained.

"Yes it is. A report can be put in at any time if foul play is suspected. For all we know Skylar may have her?"

"Dr. Stevens was released less than an hour ago. I can have local hospitals checked out before you file a report."

"Whatever. I just know something has to be done. Lex wouldn't be out of touch like this. Our daughter hasn't been out of the hospital that long. She always checks on the kids."

"I'll take care of this right now. Do you have a current picture of Alexis? I'm going to need her vehicle information also." Rick said.

Justin went into his wallet then gave Rick a picture he had of Alexis from six months ago. Then he gave Rick the make, model, color, and license plate number of Alexis' car. Rick left Justin and Darius in his office.

"I feel a little better now. I just hope my gut is wrong and there is nothing wrong with Lex." Justin said.

Harrison was so excited. He couldn't wait until Skylar arrived. He hurried to get himself cleaned up and took care of his expected guest after he got the call from Skylar that she was released and on her way over. He hated that he put himself in the position of falling in love with Skylar knowing that all she thought about was the no-good fool Darius. When he met her over a year ago he was very cold to her because he was just coming off the raw emotion of leaving WES. She arranged to bump into him three times before she approached him with a plan that would be beneficial for both of them. She knew Harrison had an axe to grind with WES and she wanted Darius back in the worse way.

Somewhere between all the meeting and planning Harrison was hooked. He knew Skylar started having sex with him six months into their relationship because that was the only way she could get him to do what she wanted. She was amazing in bed. Darius had to be a fool. The things she did to him and the way she made him feel was like nothing he had experience before. Deep in his heart he prayed that he would be able to win her heart from that fool that didn't care one bit about her. Hearing the front door open, Harrison hurried from the kitchen to meet the love of his life.

"Wow. It's so good to see you, Skylar." Harrison said with so much love in his heart.

"Don't start all that smothering. I had a lousy day."

"I knew you would be exhausted. I can run you a bath then we can eat. I made all your favorites."

"I don't have time for a bath. I will take a quick shower, grab a bite to eat then I have to go back down to the police station. They are keeping Danae on some trumped-up charges in Florida."

"Honey you need to rest. You can take care of that tomorrow."

"No I can't. They are transferring her in the morning. I'm just allow an hour visit tonight."

"I can go with you. Then we can come back here to eat and catch up."

"No what you need to do is to come up with a way to expedite our plan. I'm not waiting forever to get what I want."

"I've been thinking. I don't care about that stupid company anymore. Let's move on with our lives. Maybe we can move to Florida so we can be close to your stepsister."

"That's not going to happen. I told you more than once that my future is with Darrius."

"That's not going to ever happen. He's in love with someone else."

Skylar went across the room until she stood in front of Harrison. She slapped him hard across the face. "It will happen. I didn't come all this way to leave empty handed." Skylar left Harrison standing there with a look of rage on his face.

The Candidate: Back to Business

Chapter Twenty-Three

It was now near seven o'clock. Alexis hasn't been seen in nearly twelve hours. Rick had checked with the local hospitals but there was no sign of Alexis. He also didn't have any luck tracking down her car. Justin and Darius were still at the police station. Justin had talked to Alexis' mom and asked her to keep Allison overnight. The twins were going to spend the night at their friend's house a few doors down. Justin figure he would be in for a long night because he was determined to find Alexis. As they were walking out the door Darius stopped. Justin turned to look at him to see what was going on. Darius was looking at the woman that was walking towards them.

"DK is that her? Justin asked in a low angry voice.

"Yes." Before Darius could say anything else Justin quickly made his way to Skylar.

"Where is my wife?" Justin asked Skylar grabbing her arm.

"Get your hands off of me you crazy fool." Skylar broken free of Justin's hold and backed up then said, "Hi lover boy. Long time no see baby. How have you been?"

Darius wanted to ignore Skylar, but he knew that wasn't going to be possible. "You need to stop this craziness right now, Sky."

"I don't know what you are talking about dear."

"I asked you a question lady." Justin spoke again.

"I don't know you or your wife sir. I suggest you watch how you treat a lady you don't even know."

"I suggest you start talking before I beat the… Justin didn't get a chance to finish his statement because Rick rushed up to where they were standing then asked what was going on.

"This maniac assaulted me." Skylar said with an attitude.

"Sky you need to go on about your business." Darius said.

"I was minding my own business until the two of you showed up."

"Justin, I told you Dr. Stevens doesn't have anything to do with Alexis' disappearance." Rick said.

"Well, I think she does." Justin headed towards Skylar again. Rick told Skylar to leave and tend to her business then he slightly grabbed Justin by the arm and ushered him towards his car. Once they were in front of Justin's car Rick started talking.

"I'm working hard to find Alexis, but you have to calm down?"

"How do you expect me to do that, Rick? The longer she is missing the less chances we have to find her unharmed." Justin replied.

"Go home, Justin. I will stay here to keep things rolling. I will also put a tail on Dr. Stevens when she leaves here."

"Jus let's go back to your house. Maybe Lexie's phone was lost or something and she's at home now" Darius added.

"I'm going home, but I need you to contact me as soon as you find out what's going on."

"I'll keep you posted." Rick said as he watched Justin and Darius pull out of the parking lot.

Alexis was in her thoughts when an angry Harrison charged into the room. His face was so red she though he would explode. She didn't know what happened since he left her and now, but she knew it had to be something bad. He rushed over to stand in front of Alexis then snatched the tape off her mouth.

"You know this is all your fault."

The Candidate: Back to Business

Alexis was gathering her thoughts before she spoke again so she wouldn't anger Harrison further. "What are you blaming me for now, Harrison?"

"Ruining my life. I was willing to leave all the pettiness behind me, but I've been used by another person that doesn't have my best interest at heart."

"Who has used you and what does that has to do with me?"

"That ungrateful witch, Skylar."

Alexis wanted to be careful how she proceeded now. It seems she was about to get some answers to the questions she came to Harrison house for in the first place. "Now I know you're off base, Harrison. I don't even know that woman."

"Maybe not but your hubby bestie knows who she is."

"This is unnecessary, Harrison. Just let me go and move on with your life."

"You must think I'm a fool. I let you go you and Justin will be at the police station filing a report in no time."

"So far you haven't done anything wrong. Keep it that way by letting me go."

"You still think you in control don't you? Sitting there all tied up and you still think that you have something to bargain with."

"I understand how you feel, Harrison. You feel you were cheated out of the CEO position and the ownership at WES. Again, Justin and I had nothing to do with Ross' decisions. Justin has worked hard at WES since he got out of college."

"I have more time than that invested. On top of that WES wouldn't be what it is today if my dad hadn't bailed Ross out not once but twice."

"I don't know what you are talking about, Harrison."

"There were two different occasions when WES was about to go under. My dad not only use most of our savings, but he got investors in on the deal."

"We didn't know that Harrison."

"Ross promised my dad on his death bed that he would make sure I would always have a place at WES."

"Ross kept that promise, Harrison. He knew you were doing underhanded things in the race for the CEO seat and about how you started sabotaging the company once you loss the seat."

Harrison turned even redder before he answered, "I wouldn't had to do any of those things if the old man had kept his promised. I wasted enough time with you. Now that things have blown up in my face, I have to figure out another strategy. It won't be good for you once I put another plan in place. The next time you see me will be your last." Ross headed towards the door then started laughing to the top of his lungs. Then he turned around got the duct tape off the desk. After taping Alexis' mouth again he looked at her shook his head then walked out the door.

Alexis sat in the chair scared to death. This was the first time she felt that Harrison wasn't going to set her free. As tears rolled down her face she thought about how badly she had to use the bathroom, needed something to eat and drink but most importantly she thought about never seeing Justin and the kids again and that was the worst of all. Alexis tried to unbind her hands and feet. She wasn't going to just sit there and let Harrison take her out. She was going to think of something because there was no way she was ready to say goodbye to her family.

The Candidate: Back to Business

Chapter Twenty-Four

Justin and Darius had almost made it to Justin's house when Darius received a call from Phil. Justin didn't care about what Phil had to say right now. The only person he wanted to hear from was Alexis or Rick with news about Alexis. Turning Darius conversation out, Justin thought about what his next move should be to find his wife. He felt like he was running out of options. Running into Skylar at the police station didn't make Justin feel any better. Skylar was a very pretty woman. He understood why Darius made the bad choice of letting their relationship go too far. Until it is proven differently he still felt that Skylar had something to do with Alexis' disappearance. Justin came out of his thoughts when he heard Darius yelling into his phone at Phil. Darius told Phil they could meet at Justin's house.

"What's going on, DK?" Justin asked.

"Phil has some news to share with us. I asked him to meet us at your house."

"What kind of news?"

"It's better if he explained it to you. He'll be over in ten minutes." Darius said as he and Justin pulled into Justin's driveway. Justin was sadden there was no sign that Alexis was home. Once they were inside Justin told Darius they could meeting in his office. As they were heading back to the office the doorbell rang. Justin let Phil inside then they headed to the table that was located on the other side of the room across from the large cheery wood desk. Darius and Phil was quiet so Justin started the conservation.

"Why do I get the feeling that I'm not going to like what you about to say?"

"Jus, man you not going to believe this mess." Darius said.

"Justin I like to show you some pictures." Phil said then laid out four pictures in front of Justin.

Justin couldn't believe his eyes. "I know you're not tailing my wife."

"No of course not, but we do still have Harrison's house under surveillance."

"Hold on. You're saying these were taken at Harrison's house?"

"Yes. My guy just turned over his case file to me. I was upset and was not only late turning this over, but he left his post unattended for about an hour." Phil to a deep breath then continued. "As you can see by the date stamp Alexis arrived at Harrison's at eight forty-seven."

"Why the hell would she go over there? We agreed to give you and the police time to work this case."

"Unfortunately, my guy sat there about an hour with no activity. He left his post at eleven o'clock and when he arrived back at eleven fifty-five she had already left."

"So you're saying that Harrison's house was unattended during that time?"

"Yes. There was no more activity until Dr. Stevens arrived. She only stayed for fifty-five minutes. I'm sorry I didn't get this information earlier." Phil apologized.

Justin stood and headed for the door. "Where are you going Jus?" Darius asked.

"I know you're not asking me that question right now, DK?"

"Hold up Jus, I'm going with you." All three men left Justin's house. Phil told them he would meet them there.

Justin was driving like a mad man. All he could think about was that Alexis was in trouble. All the time that passed he didn't consider Harrison since Phil had someone posted at his house. Justin had to calm down. He couldn't get mad because the man didn't recognize Alexis or her car, but he was in a mood to be logical. He felt a little better knowing Alexis'

whereabouts for some portion of the day. When they arrived at Harrison's house he was glad they his gate was open. Justin didn't want to take Darius' advice to call Rick to let him know they were going to see Harrison. Justin said the police would make the situation worse and he wasn't taking chance on losing out of getting information from Harrison. Justin banged on the door after he didn't get a response after ringing the doorbell several times.

"Open this door right now, Harrison. I'm not leaving until I get some answers."

"Jus, man we need to get Rick involved. He can make Harrison open up."

"No he can't. Not without a warrant. I'm not waiting that long. I'm going to give you two minutes Harrison. If you don't open this door by then I'm going to break it down."

Justin's threat went unanswered for a little over two minutes then Harrison swung the door open. "What the hell do you want? You can't come over here starting trouble in my neighborhood."

"Where is my wife?" Justin asked pushing his way into Harrison's house.

"Are you crazy? You just can't burst into my house like you own it."

"I just did. Now I'm going to ask you again, where is my wife?"

"How the hell should I know? I'm not her keeper."

"She came over here at eight fifty-five this morning" Justin continued.

Harrison was taken off guard. He didn't know what to say to that so he played it off. "So, she was only here for a few minutes before I told her to get off her soapbox and get out of my house."

"Wrong again. She was here much longer than a few minutes."

"This is insane. I want both of you out of my house now?" Harrison yelled. He was so glad he made Alexis take four of his sedatives earlier.

"What did you say to her, Harrison?" Darius asked.

Ignoring Darius, Harrison said, when she left here she said she had work to do at the office. That's all I know now get out."

They were standing in Harrison's living room. Justin didn't know how else to get Harrison to talk without whipping his behind so he turned to leave but dropped his keys on the floor. When he bent down to pick them up he saw a spot of blood near the table leading to the door. All of the saddened he charged at Harrison.

"I know you weren't stupid enough to do something to my wife?"

"Get off of me. Are you crazy?"

"There is blood near that table. Now start talking quick before I beat you senseless." Justin started hitting Harrison until Darius broke them up. Phil walked in with his gun drawn.

"Call the police, DK. There is blood near that table." Justin shouted. Darius pulled out his phone to make the call. Harrison started to run to towards the back of the house by Justin stopped him. He pushed Harrison on the sofa and stood guard in front of him.

"All of you are trespassing. I'm going to have all of you locked up with the cops get here."

"If you make it until they get here. What did you do to Alexis?"

"I'm know answering anymore of your stupid questions. It's not my fault you can't keep up with your wife. Maybe she is off having a good time with a real man instead of being tie down to a thief."

"This is the last time I'm going to tell you this. I didn't steal he seat or WES from you. I earned that seat fair and square. I didn't have anything to do with Ross leaving me the company. I was as shocked as you were.

The Candidate: Back to Business

"Keep thinking that foolishness. The old man promised my dad to take care of me as far as the company was concerned."

"He tried to take care of you, Harrison. You were just too bitter to see that he was making room for you at the top."

"Yeah, but I would still be reporting to you. That wasn't going to work for me."

"That's why we are here at this moment with no resolution. I have nothing else to say to you until the police gets here." Justin stood between the living and dining room entrance so Harrison couldn't run out of the room. He didn't worry about him running out the front door because Darius and Phil were standing there.

Chapter Twenty-Five

Darius and Phil stood by Harrison's front door. They whispered to each other while Justin was dealing with Harrison. Phil had apologized to Darius more than once about the mistake his man made when he left his post unattended. The discussed anything could have happened in that time. Phil was anxious because this didn't look good for Alexis. Even though there was only a small amount of blood on Harrison's floor that blood could very well be Alexis'. The men stopped talking for a few seconds before Phil restarted the conversation.

"Darius, we have to prepare Justin for the possibility something bad happened to Alexis."

"He's not ready to hear that, Phil."

"Ready or not that unattended hour could mean that Harrison had time to harm her."

"I don't want to hear that. We need you to let us talk to the guy that was on duty. He will need to talk to the police too." Darius said. A few minutes later they could hear the sirens approaching. Darius went over to talk to Justin.

"Jus, let the police handle this. They know what they are doing."

"I don't want to hear that DK. Lex has been missing for hours and they are no closer to finding her."

"My, Justin. We're a bit touchy." Harrison said with a smirk on his face.

Justin headed towards Harrison, he got off the couch and ran towards the front door when he saw the police had arrived.

"I want all three of these men arrested for trespassing." Harrison told Rick."

Rick didn't like Harrison. He had to deal with him when his dad was alive and he worked at WES, but since both of those factors didn't exist any longer he didn't have to watch what he said for the most part.

"Hello, Harrison." Rick said.

"Don't hello me. These men burst into my house in a threatening manner. I don't want them here."

"Why don't we have a seat and talk for a few minutes." After they were seated Rick continued. "It's my understanding you may have been the last person to see Alexis."

"That's not true. She left here hours ago. I'm sure she has been in touch with someone. Like I told Justin she might just wanted to get away from him."

The officer that came in with Rick stopped Justin as he was trying to get to Harrison. "There is blood over there by the table. I know he has done something to my wife."

"That's nonsense. I cut myself earlier. I thought I cleaned it up, but I guess I didn't to a good job."

"I'm not leaving until he tells me what he's done with my wife. Rick you need to search this place from top to bottom." Justin yelled.

"No one is searching my premises. There is no probable cause."

"He's lying through his teeth. When we first arrived here he said Lex was only here for minutes when it was closer to an hour."

"I know my rights. You can't search my house without a search warrant without my permission. Guess what I don't give my permission so you all can leave now."

"Whatever." Justin said then walked towards the door to the table where he saw the blood. There was nothing else there until he looked under the table and he saw pieces of glass.

"Rick there is glass under this table. I don't like this…Justin stopped when a tall heavy-set man entered. He talked to Phil for a few minutes. Phil smiled then call Darius over to let him know what he learned.

"Mike here knows he messed up today. So after his shift he did some leg work. It seems that he got a report that Mr. Harper moved the vehicle that Alexis' arrive in this morning. It should be somewhere in the back of the house."

"I knew it. I know that should give you cause to search the place from top to bottom" Justin said anxiously.

"Is this true, Harrison?' Rick asked.

"I'm not saying another word without my attorney." Harrison said crossing his arms across his protruding stomach.

"That's you right, but we do have enough to search the premises." Rick turned to his officer then asked him to call in a search team. Since it was now dark outside, lights and other equipment would be needed. Rick gave Harrison permission to call his attorney. He told Justin when backup arrive they would search the inside of the house. Justin went over to talk to Darius, Phil, and Mike.

"Thank you, Mike. You arrived just in time. I appreciate the extra work you put into this case."

"I'm just sorry I had to leave without waiting for backup. My stomach was acting up, so I had to find a restroom."

"If that's all you need, Darius, Mike and I will take our leave. I'll be in touch with you tomorrow." Phil said.

"Thanks, Phil. So you're sure Skylar is at the house." Darius asked.

"Yes. I'm headed over there right now to relive my guy. I will be taking over the night shift."

"Cool. Talk to you tomorrow." Darius went back over to where Rick and Harrison were sitting once Phil and Mike left.

"If there is something you want to tell us now is the time." Justin said to Harrison. The look Harrison gave to Justin was pure hate, but he didn't say a word.

"How long before the search team arrive?" Justin asked.

"They are less than ten minutes out. Maybe it's best the two of you head home. I will keep you posted." Rick responded.

"There is no way I'm leaving. I know Lexie is in trouble and the answers lies here."

"Well, you two will have to wait in the car. You can't be in here when we search the premises."

"Fine." Justin and Darius left the house but refused to leave the premises. Justin have been beside himself since he saw the blood on Harrison floor. His gut was telling him it was Alexis'.

Chapter Twenty-Six

Justin and Darius were sitting in the car waiting on the search party to arrive at Harrison's house. They were talking about the next project WES would take on since things have quiet down from Darius' therapy sessions. Justin was proud of how Darius handled that situation with all that was going on in his personal and business life. Justin needed to take his mind of what was going on with Alexis. Both Justin and Darius nearly jumped out of their skin when Phil rushed up to the passenger side of Justin's car where Darius was sitting.

"Come on man we have to go." Phil said in a hurried voice.

"What's going on, Phil?" Darius asked.

"Dr. Stevens slipped past my man. She is holding Ciara hostage at the house where she has been living.

"You got to be kidding me. What kind of fools do you have on your staff that they can't do their jobs?" Darius asked. "Jus, man I'm sorry, but I have to go. Keep me posted."

"No problem, DK. You do the same." Justin replied as he watched Darius hurry behind Phil to his car.

Justin didn't know if he was supposed to call the police or not. To be on the safe side he decided he better do it so Darius wouldn't take any foolish changes. The he thought about not having the exact address. He had it in the report that Phil gave to Darius. Darius had made him a copy, but the report was at his office and there was no way he was leaving there until after Harrison's house is thoroughly searched. Once he finished that thought he saw the flashing lights from the back up vehicles. There were two police cars and a police truck. Justin began to panic when he saw the EMS pull in behind the police truck. As he was about to get out of his car Rick called.

"Justin, you need to leave the premises so that the search party can do their jobs. Harrison will be taken and guarded in one of the patrol cars." Rick said in a rush.

"That's not going to happen. Were you able to get anything else out of Harrison?" Justin asked.

"No. He has uttered one word since you left out the door. This is not a request Justin this is an order. I don't want to have one of my men arrest you." Rick continued.

Justin became angry. "Where the hell you expect me to go?"

"Go home, Justin."

"And do what. Worried about if my wife is alive or dead" Justin calmed down for a moment. "You need to send help over to Skylar's house she has taken Ciara hostage."

"Great. I thought you guys had her under surveillance?"

"She slipped the detail. Why didn't you have someone on her with all that is going on?" Justin asked.

"We didn't have proof she was involved. I couldn't order a detail to be put on her with probable cause."

"I'll leave but I'm only going around the corner so I can be close by when your team is done with their search."

"I'll let you know when the search is over. I have to go now. We are about to search the inside of the house while the search party is taking care of the outside. You are going to have to be patient. It's dark out there and Harrison refused to turn on the outside lights."

"Make sure you let me know as soon as your guys are done." Justin ended the call. He left Harrison's house and parked one street over.

By the time Darius and Phil reached Skylar's house the police were already there. They told them they could be there. Rick told them he was a private investigator, and he has been tailing Skylar. He was told he and Darius had to vacate because this was a police matter now that she had taken a hostage. Darius wasn't having it.

"I'm not going anywhere. She has my girl and there. That chic is out of her mind." Darius shouted.

"We know this is a serious situation. She knocked out one of our officers and took her uniform." The office explained.

"So that is how she slipped by my man." Phil said.

"She became upset when we wouldn't let her see her stepsister then caused a scene. We made her leave, but she was able to slip back in."

"I need to talk to her. She is doing all of this because she in delusional. She thinks she and I have a relationship. She told my girl we were married." Darius added.

"Sorry be we can't let any civilians get involved. Our negotiator will be here in less than five minutes."

"Come on Darius we have to go." Phil said.

"No. I will be able to talk her down."

The officer looked at Darius then asked, "What is your relationship to the pert?" The officer asked.

"She was my therapist when I lived in Florida a while back. She followed me here." Darius didn't want to tell too much of the situation. He still felt embarrassed.

"So I take it that you two had more than a professional relationship?" The officer continued.

Feeling uncomfortable Darius was quiet for a few sections before he spoke again, "We were together only one time. She followed me back, set up residence in this house, and has been causing problems in both my personal and business life."

"Wow that was you she was going on and on about. She said she married a man who thought he could get away from her by leaving the state."

This was the last thing that Darius wanted to hear. "Unfortunately that is me you heard about." Two patrol cars pulled up.

"On second thought. You guys need to leave the vicinity but stay close by. We may need you Mr. Kane."

Darius looked at the office as he and Rick were leaving. It was a shame that he knew Darius' name without him mentioning it.

Chapter Twenty-Seven

Justin had dosed off. He was exhausted. He talked to Alexis' mom again to check on Allison. She was sound asleep. He had to tell her there was no news about Alexis's whereabouts. He did tell her everything that was going on at Harrison's. Far away he heard a phone ringing he was so tired he couldn't get to it to answered it. It stops ring so he relaxed. A few minutes later it started ringing again. Justin jumped when he finally woke up and saw that he had missed two calls from Rick. Dialing Rick's number Justin didn't give him a chance to say a word.

"Have you found Lex?"

"Yes we did." Rick answered

Justin became nervous when Rick didn't say anything else. "Is she alright?"

"Where are you, Justin?"

"A block over behind Harrison house."

"Stay there I'm coming to get you." Rick ended the call before Justin could say anything else. Rick picked Justin up and told him they needed to go to the hospital.

"What is wrong with Lex, Rick?'

"I need you to stay calm. We found her tied up in a chair in one of the bedrooms down in the basement."

Justin was horrified. "You didn't answer my question. Is she alright?"

"I don't know, Justin. She never regained consciousness while the EMT's were working on her."

"I'm going to kill him." Justin said in a cold steely voice.

"Stop talking crazy, Justin. We are going to go to the hospital, and you going to take care of your wife and leave Harrison to the authorities."

Justin didn't say a word. Ten minutes later they were at the hospital. Since he was with Rick they were able to use the EMS entrance. Once they were at the front desk Justin started talking.

"Where is my wife, Alexis Bradley?"

"Hold on a second sir. I have to finish this call." The nurse said.

Justin snacked the phone out of the nurse hand then hung it up. "I'm going to ask you again. Where is my wife?"

"Cut it out, Justin." Rick said then looked at the nurse's name tag. "Sorry about that Nurse Wilson. Alexis Bradley should have arrived about half hour or so ago."

The nurse rolled her eyes at Justin then turned to answered Rick once she looked on her chart for Alexis' name. "Mrs. Bradley is in Room 4. I will call back there to see if someone can come to get you all."

"Thank you, Nurse Wilson." Rick and Justin went to the waiting room to wait for someone to come and get them.

"Tell me what happened, Rick."

"After thoroughly checking the first two floors in the house coming up empty we headed to the basement. There were two bedrooms down there. One was unlocked and we came up clean. The second bedroom was locked. We attempted to get the key from Harrison, but he still refused to cooperate." Taking a deep breath Rick continued, "We had to break the door down. As we moved further into the room where we found Alexis with her hands and feet bound together with duct tape. Her mouth was also taped."

"Oh my God." That was all Justin was able to say when a nurse came into the waiting room calling out Bradley family. The waiting room was half full.

"Hi. I'm Justin Bradley. How is my wife doing?"

"She is asleep right now. She has been through an ordeal. There were no signs of physical trauma outside the knot on the back of her head where she said she was hit from behind with a lamp."

Justin was uncomfortable with asking, but he needed to know. "Was she sexually assaulted?"

"No she has been thoroughly examined. She was awake for only a few minutes. With what she has been through the doctor gave her a sedative so she could sleep."

"Can I see her?"

"Sure follow me." As the nurse and Justin was walking away Rick stopped him.

"You stay here with Lexie. I'm going to check on the situation with Dr. Stevens."

"Sure. Tell DK, I'll be in touch tomorrow." When Justin got to Alexis' room, he was so happy to see that she didn't have any injuries that he could see. She just looks like she was having a peaceful sleep. He couldn't wait to get his hands on Harrison. Harrison was going to regret the day he was born after he finished with him. This petty fool did all this to his wife over a stupid company that he would have eventually run into the ground if he had been put in charge. He had no idea how to treat people. Most of WES employees feared him more than they respected him. Justin didn't want to think about any of that right now. All he was concerned with was having his wife back. He will call her mother in the morning since it was so late to fill her in and to ask if she and the nanny could keep Allison and the twins for a few days to give Alexis a chance to get stronger. He was happy when the nurse said if there were no complications that Alexis would be able to go home in the morning.

The Candidate: Back to Business

Chapter Twenty-Eight

Darius and Phil went back to Phil's car that was parked near Skylar's house. Darius didn't want to leave the scene. He wanted to be as close as possible to Ciara. The officer they communicated with told them to leave once the negotiator arrived. Phil thought this was a good time to tell Darius what the process would be from here on out since the negotiator was there. Just as Phil was ready to tell Darius the next steps they saw Rick pulling in towards Skylar's house. He was alone, so Darius jumped out the car to find out why Justin wasn't with him.

"Hey, Rick. Where is Justin?"

"He's at the hospital. I don't have long to talk, but we found Alexis. She was bound in the basement in one of Harrison's bedrooms. Harrison has been arrested." Rick explained.

"Oh my God. Is Lexie okay?"

"Physically yes. The doctor said she was going to be okay, but mentally she has been through a horrifying ordeal."

I'll go see Jus as soon as you guys can get Ciara safely away from that nut case."

"He said he will talk to you later. Since you have personal knowledge of Dr. Stevens we will need you to stay close by."

"Sure thing." Darius headed back to the car where Phil was waiting. "Lexie is at the hospital and Harrison has been arrested."

"Wow. We halfway through this case. Before you left I was going to tell you what is likely to play out since they have the Captain and negotiator here."

"I wish I could go to the hospital to be with Jus and Lexie, but I'm worried sick about how frighten Ciara must be right now."

"This is all such a mess. The first few hours of a hostage taking is critical. They probably will need you to tell them whatever you can about Dr. Stevens personality and why she is so angry at Ciara."

"Because she's nuts and delusional. We never had a relationship, but she had the nerve to tell Ciara that we're married."

"I'm sure the police already know she's messed up in the head.' Phil said with a slight smile on his face. "Since she is obsessed with you this doesn't look good for Ciara. Especially since we know she is armed."

"I remember one time when I told her I was moving back to Michigan she said she would kill herself if I left her."

"I'm wondering if she intended on taking Ciara hostage. If not this also could spell trouble. The Chief isn't going to get anywhere with her. She is holding a grudge against him because of Danae. The negotiator will have to build a rapport with her. That is where you going to come into play."

"I wish I didn't have to deal with that crazy heifer. Once I stopped being her patient she became unglued because I didn't want to see her at all."

"We have to wait to see what she wants. She may have impossible demands. I will bet my last dollar that you are going to be par of her demand."

"I would change places with Ciara in a heartbeat. Her life shouldn't be in danger because I had a brief fling with a crazy person."

"I don't want to scare you man, but if she gets you in there we're going to be dealing with a murder/suicide situation."

Darius thought for moment. "I will still change places with Ciara if it comes to that. Now that I think about it this may have been Sky's plan all along. She knows I will never have a relationship with her. Some of what she's doing is the same things I went through with Roslyn. My guess she wants this to end just like it did at the press conference." Darius stopped talking when his phone started to ring with an unknown number. He though I may be Justin calling from the hospital.

"Hi lover boy." Skylar said before Darius could utter a word.

Just hearing her voice gave Darius the chills. "Let Ciara go, Sky. She has nothing to do with our situation." Darius said calmly.

"I beg to differ. She is a homewrecker. If you want to see her stay in one piece tell those fools out there to leave." Skylar ended the call before Darius could say another word.

"This is unreal. She has no intention of letting Ciara get of there alive. I need to go talk to Rick." Darius left Phil's car and headed over to the house where Rick and others were parked.

It was almost seven o'clock in the morning. Justin was still with Alexis. She hadn't wakened up all night. He was morning to get her to update her mom and Darius on all that has happened. Plus he wanted to know how the situation was going with Skylar and Ciara. Justin always been a light sleeper so when Alexis was moaning he woke up and rushed to her bed. His body was aching trying to sleep on the small cot they gave him earlier. He grabbed Alexis' hand then started saying comforting words to her. He was so happy after a few minutes she opened her big beautiful brown eyes.

"Hello sleeping beauty." Justin said quietly.

"What happened? Where am I?" Alexis tried to move but the pain in her head was killing her.

"You're in the hospital, Lex. Try not to talk. You need to rest." It seemed like the words worked her magic. Alexis closed her eyes and went back to sleep. Since Alexis was asleep, Justin left her room quietly to call to give a report to her mom. After giving her all the details Alexis' dad agreed to pick up the boys and take them to the house to pack closed for the twins and Alexis. He told her mom he would be over later that day to talk to the boys to let them know what was going on. He asked her not to let them watch TV is case they run a story on Harrison. After getting a bit to eat he called Darius.

"Morning, DK. How is things going over there?"

"It's been hours with hardly any change. Sky called me a brief moment one time and the negotiator was able to get her on the phone long enough for her to tell them to go to hell and that she will tell them when she gets ready what her demands are. How is Lexie?"

"She woke up for a few minutes. She is resting. I filled her mom in on everything and her day is going to pick up the twins so they could pack a few things to stay over there for a few days. I'm so glad they are on summer break."

"That's good. You will get the chance to focus on Lexie. I'm glad Phil let me his car. He had one of his guys to pick him up a few hours in the standoff."

"I can't wait to all this is over. I wonder what it's going to take to break Skylar."

Darius was quiet for a few seconds then said, "Jus, I know exactly what it's going to take. You're not going to like this, but I told Rick to let me go in there to take Ciara's place."

"Man I know you're joking. That won't end well at all. She knows you're not going to be with her. If you are going in there all three of you aren't going to leave there alive."

"That's exactly what Rick said, but I have to do something."

"They are trained for situations like this. Let them do they jobs and you chill out." Justin didn't want to lose his best friend. He felt like he lost a part of himself when Darius moved to Florida.

"I have to go, Jus. The negotiator is signaling for me to come over. Tell Lexie I love her, and you take care."

"Will do. Stay safe, DK." Justin ended the call then headed back to Alexis's room.

Chapter Twenty-Nine

Darius headed back to the truck where Rick and the negotiator were working from. From the looks on their faces he wasn't going to like what they had to say. It had been almost eighteen hours. They seemed to be getting nowhere with Skylar. They warned him it may be a while before they gotten any results.

"Do you have any news?" Darius asked.

"Yes. Dr. Stevens picked up the phone again. She said she is ready to tell us what she wants. She wanted you to be here when she tell us her demands." Rick stated.

"Okay. I'm ready." Darius said.

The negotiator called Skylar. She waited to the fourth ring before she answered. "Is he there?" Skylar asked.

The negotiator nodded so Darius answered. "I'm here Sky. Is Ciara okay?"

"Stop talking and all of you listen. The homewrecker better that she should be. She doesn't have any idea of what shut your damn mouth means."

"You better not hurt her, Sky." Darius said. He was starting to lose his cool.

"You're not in charge here lover boy. Now shut up and listen. All of you. I'm a reasonable person. I don't want to be around the homewrecker any longer than I have to. So here's the deal. I have a three for one offer. The homewrecker will be set free when I get the three people on my list here."

This time the negotiator spoke up. "We're listening Dr. Stevens."

"The first person is you lover boy. I want you, Danae, and Harrison in exchange for the homewrecker."

Everyone was quiet for a moment. The negotiator knew he couldn't tell her no, but there was no way they were going to send any civilian inside. Danae was in the process of being extradited to Florida and Harrison was being held on a twenty-four-hour suicide watch.

"This could be arranged, but it may take a while." The negotiator said calmly.

"Time is running out for the homewrecker. If I had to hear another word come out of her lying mouth I'm not going to be responsible for what happens next." Skylar ended the call after making that statement.

"I was prepared to offer myself, but I wonder what she want with Harrison and Danae?" Darius said out loud but not talking to them directly.

"We're not going to be able to give in to her demands. Danae is on her way to Florida and Harrison is being held on a twenty-four-hour suicide watch." Rick explained.

"We have to do as she says. You can tell she is slipping further into her on little deranged world." Darius didn't want to hear that they had no intentions on complying with her demands.

"We can't take that chance, Darius." Rich stated firmly.

"Okay let's comprise with her. I think she would let Ciara go if she had me."

"We told you before that we can't let you do that."

"Are you all just going to let her kill Ciara? We all know that is what going to happen if we don't agree with her terms."

"We still have time. She can't hurt the hostage because then she would lose her bargaining tool." The negotiator explained.

"Everyone is tired. This can't go on much longer. I'm going to do this with our without your approval." Darius said then walked out. Ciara had been awake for a few hours. She was upset at herself for letting her guard down giving Skylar the upper hand. After her mail appointment, she finished running a few errands so she could catchup with Justin and Darius to see how the search for Alexis was going. She called Alexis' phone twice without getting an answer after speaking to Justin and Darius. When she arrived home, she was putting her groceries away then glance out the window to her backyard and saw that she had left the water hose out. She knew she had to put it up because every blue moon her neighbor's dog gets into her yard. One time he had a field day with her hose and put several holes in it. After she was done putting up her groceries she went out to her back to take care of her hose before it got darker (it was already dusk dark). She wrapped the hose around it holder then proceeded to take the hose to it resting place in her garage. She heard something behind her but before she could turn around, someone grabbed her from behind. She felt something go across her face then everything went dark.

When Ciara regained consciousness hours later she was looking into the face of the one person she wished she would never meet, Skyler. She recognized Skyler because of the many times Darius made sure to would know who she was if the happened to meet. Still a little groggy, she was trying to focus on Skyler's face. Although Skyler had a very beautiful, face the evil smirk that was on it made her look unattractive.

"Well, what do we have here?" Skyler asked.

Looking around at her surroundings, Ciara asked, "Where am I?"

"That's not important." Skyler answered.

Thinking to herself, Ciara wished she had waited to put that hose away since it was getting dark outside. "What do you want, Skyler?"

"I see you're acquainted with me."

"You still haven't answered my question."

"You're not in a position to demand any answers from me." Skyler said in a nasty voice.

That is when Ciara noticed her hands and feet were bound. The rope was tied tight and was sitting in a recliner that was in a living room. "You're not going to get away with this, Skyler. Where is Alexis?"

"How should I know? I don't have a beef with her. You're going to have to talk to that nut case Harrison for that one."

Wow. How in the world could this woman have the nerve to call anyone a nut case? "You shouldn't have a beef with me. I haven't done anything to you."

This statement angered Skyler even further. She went in stood and front of Ciara then slapped her hard across her face. "You're going to lie to my face?" Skylar started pacing around the living room floor then she came back to stand in front of Ciara. "You're the reason why my husband came back to this God-awful state."

Trying to stay calm even though her face was hurting, Ciara said, Darius did not come back for me. He needed a new start after his parents passed away. He also missed his best friend and his old job."

"Bullshit. I had him all to myself after his parents died. We were happy."

"When Darius first arrived back in town I was going through a divorce. We were not seeing each other. We were acquainted through Alexis." Ciara tried to explain.

"Don't lie to me. You were going out with him for a while flaunting and throwing yourself at a married man. You should be ashamed of yourself.

Ciara didn't have too much to say to that. She did start dating Darius before the ink was completely dry on her divorce papers. "I was under the impression he was single. He said he's never been married."

"There is more to marriage than a piece of paper. That is what's wrong with women like you. You take what's not yours for the taking." Skylar yelled then began to pace the floor again. Then she said, "Just shut up. I'm tired of hearing your voice. Skylar then grabbed a rag that was sitting near Ciara to bind her mouth.

The Candidate: Back to Business

Chapter Thirty

Justin was taking a nap. He was exhauster, but he had to be there when Alexis woke up. He was a little concerned because the doctor said she should be awake by now. He was able to talk to the twins earlier that afternoon. He promised them he would be over to their grandparents' house that day to let them know what is going on. He also talked to Darius again who was frustrated. They hadn't gotten any closer to rescuing Ciara. Justin was amazed at Skylar's demands. In his mind all he could think about was that Skylar had no intentions of freeing Ciara. It was clear to him now since she asked for Darius, Harrison, and Danae it was her plan to setting her beef with them once and for all. Justin could feel himself moving and that someone was watching him. He slowly opened his eyes then say it was Alexis looking at him. He moved closer to her bed so he could talk to her.

"Oh my God. It's so wonderful to see your pretty brown eyes." Justin said to his smiling wife.

"Hey, Jus. What happened to me?" Alexis asked softly.

"That's a long story. We can talk about that later. How are you feeling?

"Like my head been bashed in."

"Do you need me to get the doctor? You also have a drip if you need it for pain."

"No doctor. I'm trying to remember but everything is so fuzzy."

"Don't worry about that, Lex. There is plenty of time to talk about what's been going on."

"I can see I'm in a hospital. How long have I've been here?

"Overnight. You sound like you need some rest. Don't worry about anything. Just rest your eyes."

"I need to know…That was all Alexis could get out before she went back to sleep. An hour later the doctor said he should go home and rest because Alexis will be out the rest of the night. He didn't want to leave, but he wanted to change clothes and go see the boys. He also wanted to go over to check on Ciara. Justin knew as soon as Alexis hear about Ciara's situation she will be trying to get out of the bed to go over there.

Justin went home to take a shower. He also packed Allison and the twins' additional clothes in case they have to stay longer than a few days. He was going to have to prepare for a fight with the kids especially Jeremy. He didn't like to be from home for too long even when they were down the street with their friends. Justin going to tell them less as possible. He want to tell them the full story when they are all at home. Arrived at Alexis' parents' house, Justin took a deep breath be knocked on the door.

"Well hello, Justin. I hope you're here to talk to the twins. They are asking nonstop questions on top of being ready to go home."

"I bet they are. How are you doing, Ms. Mae?" Justin looked at Mae Miller, Alexis' mom. He was going to have a good idea how Alexis and Allison will look later in life. All three of them had skin as smooth and creamy as butter.

"I so relieved my baby girl is on the mend. I can't wait to see her." Mae responded.

"Unfortunately, we're going to have to wait until tomorrow. The doctor she needs to rest the rest of the night.

"I understand. You better head to the family room to visit the kids. I'm surprised they didn't hear you come in."

"Sure thing." Justin followed Mae to the family room and was there for two hours before he could calm the kids down.

Justin headed over to the hostage situation after leaving the kids. He wanted to get over there sooner because Rick was blowing his phone up telling him if he didn't come to get Darius under control he was going to lock him up. Justin imagined that Rick would be at the end of his rope with Darius. Darius could be uncompromising at times. He also found out on his way over that Phil was faring any better. Justin smiled at himself. He was going to have to give Sage a raise. She was holding down the office along with Tucker, Ryan, and Kristen. Pulling up to the patrol truck, Justin saw Darius sitting in a small huddle next to the negotiator and Rick.

"Jus, what are you doing here?" Darius was so happy to see his friend.

"Looks like I'm going to be saving you from lockup."

Darius glanced at the negotiator and Rick. "Ciara could have been out of there by now if they would just listen to me."

"DK. You have to let them do their jobs. They have experience in these types of situations."

"You still didn't answer my question. What are you doing her? I didn't think wild horses would drag you away from Lexie."

"They kind of threw me out. They said she would be sleep for the rest of the night. I'm just coming from her parents' house getting grilled by the kids."

"You should go home and go to sleep, Jus. One of us have to go into the office?"

"The office is fine. Sage has everything under control."

"Is Lexie going to be okay?"

"Yes. She should only be there another day or two. I had to come to get some answers. When find out about Ciara she is going to try to leave the hospital. I'm praying she doesn't hear about it since she doesn't watch TV."

"Good luck with that one. You know how much the nurses talk."

"DK, I need to run something by you." Justin said so Darius followed him out of the patrol truck.

When they got outside by Justin's car Darius said, "I'm not leaving, Jus. I know Rick has probably cried on your shoulder. They know I'm their best bet to get Ciara out of there alive.|

"I need you to be prepared, DK. This has been going on a long time. Skylar has to sleep sometime so in the state of mind she's in no telling what she might do to Ciara."

"I know. That's all I could think about. Why do you think she want Danae and Harrison here?"

"I don't want to be negative, but I think she is trying to stage a scenario similar to Roslyn's."

"That cross my mind. I still think I will be able to talk her into letter Ciara out if I trade myself." Darius didn't finish his statement because and unexpected Sage came charging towards them.

"What are you doing here, Sage? It's too dangerous for you to be out here."

"Cut the bull boss. I just hear about the whereabouts of this incident. You won't believe our good luck."

"We're listening." Darius said.

"I know this house like the back of my hand." Sage said.

"What does that have to do with this situation?" Darius wanted to know.

"I need to talk to the police. If they can visibly see Skylar then there is a secret passage at the back of the house. I can draw them a map."

"I'll go get Rick." Darius left Justin and Sage talking while he went to get Rick. This is the first time since the ordeal happened that he felt Ciara was going to be okay.

The Candidate: Back to Business

Chapter Thirty-One

Everything happened fast after Sage arrived. Rick and his fellow officers were ecstatic that Sage may have found a way in without alerting Skylar. This was still going to keep tricky. The negotiator agreed that Darius could play the part of keeping Skylar busy while Rick and the officers get into place. The plan was for Rich and three officers to go around to the back yard to locate the secret panel. It was narrow so they would have to go down one at a time. They will signal when they are in place then that's when Darius will try to make an attempt to call Skylar for a trade-off between her and Ciara. After about six rings Skylar picked up.

"Didn't I tell you not to call me until you're ready to answer my demands?"

"Sky it's me. How are you doing?" Darius said.

"Don't you dare pretend to care about me?" All you care about is this skinny heifer in that is getting on my last nerve."

"That's not true, Sky. I've been concerned about you. I don't want anyone to get hurt."

"Tell that load a bull to somebody that cares. I just decided I'm sick of waiting on you guys playing around. I'm going to show you guys I mean business." No Skylar was screaming into the phone.

"There is no need to do anything at this moment. How about we come up with another deal?" Darius tried reasoning with Sky.

"Stop wasting my time lover boy. I'm giving you fools ten minutes to meet my demands or lights out for this pretty lady." Skylar laugh with an evil expression on her face then she ended the call.

Darius went on the other side of the truck pacing then he came back to stand in front of the negotiator. "I told you that wasn't going to work. When she said we only have ten minutes she means exactly what she said."

"We can't run in there half cock. If we do that it won't end well."

"On what planet do you think it's going to end well if we keep waiting?"

"The Chief has a viable plan to get inside so we can sneak up on her. You going to have to call her again to keep her distracted."

Thinking for a few minutes, Darius called Skyler again. "You didn't give me a chance to present my deal, Sky.

"Does it entail my demands?"

"Yes, partially."

"No deal. You're wasting time. You only have eight minutes left."

"They're working on it, Sky. How about this. We can do an even exchange. I'll come in and you let Ciara come out."

"Nope. I need all three of you here so I can finish taking care of business."

"What business do we have, Sky?"

"You're find out when they get here. I'm exhausted after handling the help load on putting this plan together with the two empty brained fools."

"So you were behind the newspaper leak?" Darius asked.

"Who else. The two just got in my way. For a big time business man Harrison got whipped into action rather quickly."

"Why didn't you just come for me? No one else had anything to do with this mess."

"Liar." Then they heard Sky smack Ciara. "We have a few minutes left to play this game. Every time you lie to me your little fiend here will reap the consequences."

Darius stood there not knowing what to say. Skylar is crazy. No matter what he say she is going to find a way to turn it around on Ciara.

"Oh I see the cat got your tongue?"

"Sky, we can work this out between us. I'm sorry I didn't realize how badly I hurt you?"

"Too little too late. I will have the final say. I trusted the three of you and all of played me for a fool."

"This is between you and me. I will come in right now. Just let Ciara out."

"That time has passed. She needs to know not to come between true loves? The real women of this world need to wake up and make these homewreckers pay for destroying their happy home. You all are down to fives and counting."

"Let me know come, Sky."

"Sure, but she is staying. Hey maybe we can have a threesome."

"I'm going to kill you, you crazy b....Darius didn't finish his last statement. Before Sky hung up.

Darius walked pass the negotiator. He was headed towards Justin but kept walking. Justin grabbed Darius from behind. "You can't do this, DK."

"What else am I supposed to do?"

What happened next was unreal. The sound of gunfire coming from the inside of the house was loud. Officers and the negotiator worked on getting everyone to safety. Darius broke free from the officers and headed towards the house before anyone could stop him. A few seconds later Darius felled to the ground

It was a madhouse at the hospital. The emergency room was crowded and nosey. Rick worked with several officers to get things under control. They couldn't believe what happened when they went into the house in search of Skylar. The diagram of the secret passageway was excellent. Rick and his team were able to make their way into the house without alerting Skylar. Two officers stayed in the back of the house to make sure there wasn't anyone else in there with Skylar and Ciara. Rick and another officer headed towards the front of the house where they heard Skylar screaming into the phone at Darius. As they inched closer they were able to see Skylar standing by the window and Ciara tied up in the recliner.

Rick whispered to the officer, "We're going to let her play the phone call out then see what her next move will be." They waited for the next move.

Skylar was mad when she ended the call with Darius. She walked over then stood in front of Ciara. "This is all your fault. He has absolutely no interest in any longer." Skylar snacked the tape all Ciara's mouth.

Ciara's mouth and face was hurting. Both felt like they were swollen. "I get it now. I'm sorry I interfered with you and Darius' relationship. Let's just all move on."

"It's not that simple. I have no trust in him now. You've ruined everything."

"Please, I'm sorry..." Skylar smacked Ciara hard across the face again.

"Too little too late. I have scores to settle with all of you. You all are going too rued the day you messed over me."

Rick could see that Skylar was losing control. She paced back and forth across the floor all the while yelling at Ciara. Ciara couldn't do anything but sit there and listen. Then they heard a noise outside. Skylar ran near the window and peeked out of it. She must had thought that they were coming in because she hurried back to where Ciara was sitting, but she caught a glance at someone in the next room. Realizing she didn't have much of a chance Skylar pulled her trigger back then gunfire could be heard coming from different directions.

Now at the hospital it was shocking that more people didn't get hurt. There was only one causality, Skylar. Ciara was grazed in the head by the shot Skylar fired at her. One of the officers were hit in the upper back shoulder that were fired from one of the two officers that were checking out the back of the house. Then there was Darius. There were so many shots fired by Rick and the three officers several of them exit out of the living room window. Two of those shots hit Darius in his upper arm and chest. He was still in surgery and had lost a lot of blood. Justin had finally made it to the hospital and found Rick.

"Where is DK?"

"He is still in surgery. Come with me." Rick took Justin on the other side of the room. "I'm going to be straight with you, Justin. It's not looking good. He took a bullet to his arm and upper chest."

"What the hell happened in there, Rick?"

"Skylar was losing control. We had to move in when we got the change."

"I'm not understanding this. She had just gotten off the phone with DK. She didn't seem like she was any more out of control than she had been since the standoff."

"Something spooked her outside. She started packing. She heard one of my men on the inside then she went over to Ciara and was able to fire off a short before we took her down."

"Oh my God. How is Ciara?"

"She's going to be okay. The bullet glazed her head."

"This is a nightmare." Justin stopped what he was saying to answer his phone. He prayed the kids were okay because it was Mae calling.

"Justin where are you?" Mae asked before Justin could say anything.

"I'm at the hospital. DK and Ciara have been shot. Ciara is going to be okay, but DK is still in surgery."

"I'm sorry to hear that, but the nurse has been trying to reach you. Alexis needs you."

"Oh no. I'm about to go see her right now. I'll keep you posted. Justin ended the call with Mae. "I have to go see Lex. I know you have to be exhausted. If you leave could you have one of your men stationed here to keep an eye on DK?" Justin was headed on his way to see Alexis when Phil walked in.

"How is he, Justin?"

"Not good. Can you hang out for a while I have to go check on my wife. I don't want to leave DK unattended even though Rick said he will post someone on him."

"No problem. I'm not going anywhere. This is the first time I ever had to cases come together like this. We're going to have some trying times ahead."

"I'll be back as soon as I can." Justin left Phil in the waiting room. He was worried about Alexis. She was supposed to be out the rest of the night. This was going to be another long night.

The Candidate: Back to Business

Chapter Thirty-Two

Justin woke up the next morning the same way he had the previous morning. Alexis was just watching him sleep. The difference between this morning and yesterday morning was that Alexis had gotten her color back. She looked refresh. She looks totally different from the person he walked in on last night. That person was crying and angry. Justin was to rest just a little while longer so instead of going over there to chat with his wife he decided to think back to what happened last night when he arrived in her room.

"Jus where have you been?"

"Lex it's so good to see you awake. I didn't expect you to wake up to the morning."

"You didn't answer my question."

"Honey I went to see the kids and to let your parents know how you were doing." Justin said evasively.

"I heard the news, Justin."

Then Justin looked up at the TV that was on but the volume was down. He told the nurses not to let Alexis look at the TV if she happened to wake up. *"Honey I need you to calm down."*

"Don't tell me to calm down. Why didn't you let me know what was going on?"

"I was told you would be sleeping the rest of the night. I was going to fill you in on everything when I came in this morning."

"Give me my clothes."

"You can't leave. You may be well enough to leave in a day or two."

"I'm leaving now. Is Ciara here?"

"Yes. She going to be okay. They are just going to keep her overnight for observations."

"I want to see this for myself." Alexis stood from the bed and would have fell on the floor if Justin didn't catch her. He helped her back in bed. "Take me to her right now Jus."

"I can't do that, Lex. You need to rest."

Alexis started to move around in the bed. Then the machines started going off. Two nurses came into the room then gave her a sedative.

Now back to the present, Justin looked at Alexis and knew that he was in for a hard time.

"That was a cheap shot you pulled last night." Alexis said with a frown on her face and her arms folded.

"Morning." That was all that Justin said as he made his way over to Alexis's bed from the cot he had been sleeping on.

"I've washed up. I'm still a little weak, but I expect you to take me to Ciara's room right now."

"We have to wait for the doctor."

"He's already been here. I let you sleep because I know you are exhausted, but I want to go now."

"Give me a minute. I have to find out what's going on."

"No need. I have her room number all you have to do is get a wheelchair."

All of the sudden a sad look crossed Justin's face. "Okay. Let me wash my face. We have to go check on DK first."

"Why. Isn't he with Ciara?" Alexis asked confused.

"No he was hit twice. They don't know if he's going t make it." Justin went into the bathroom to freshen up. When he returned Alexis was sitting up in the bed with tears running down her face.

"Jus, I'm so sorry. When didn't you tell me?"

"I'll be back with the wheelchair." Justin left the room. He returned with the wheelchair then he and Alexis headed down to ICU.

Justin and Alexis went into the waiting room in ICU where Phil was sitting on the chair watching the morning news. They found out that Darius was out of surgery but was still in critical condition. Since Phil wasn't family they wouldn't tell him anything. Justin left Alexis sitting with Phil when he went to the front desk to get in touch with the doctor. They pretty much told Justin the same thing they told Phil. Justin explained that he was the closest thing Darius had to family and plus he had his medical proxy. They said once he produces it they will be able to let him know what is going on. Justin had to call Sage to ask her to go by their HR department to get the proxy. Half hour later Sage was at the hospital. While Justin was talking to the doctor Sage joined Alexis and Phil in waiting room.

Alexis started crying as soon as she saw Sage. She felt horrible getting on Justin about Ciara when Darius was in so much trouble. "I can't believe how badly I treated Jus this morning."

"What are you talking about? How are you feeling?" Sage asked.

"I have a slight headache other than that I'm fine."

"So what are you talking about treating Justin badly."

"I didn't know about Darius. He didn't tell me last night, so I was getting on him about not taking me to see Ciara last night."

Sage gave Alexis the look she used to give Alexis when she first started dating Justin. She didn't like Alexis at all. "Why on earth didn't you wait to give him a chance to explain?"

"I was just so worried about Ciara when one of the nurse told me what was going on. She only told me about Ciara."

"You need to get your act together. Darius lost a lot of blood Justin was broken hearted because they wouldn't let him ride to the hospital with Darius."

"I know Sage." Alexis wheeled her chair over towards Justin when he came into the room. The look on his face broke her heart.

"DK is still in recovery. He had a blood transfusion. They still say its touch and go. The bullet in his upper left should went straight through. The other bullet pierced his lung. He had trouble breathing and had to have a blood transfusion. They are going to carefully monitor him."

"Jus, do you want to go into the chapel and pray?" Alexis asked.

"No. We can go see Ciara then find out if you're getting out today. If so we can go pick up the kids or you can stay over to your parents. I have to go to the office for a few hours then I'm coming back up her to check on DK." Justin and Alexis went back to the waiting room with Sage and Phil.

"I appreciate the two of you being here. I will keep you posted Phil. I was just telling Lex that DK isn't out of the woods yet."

"No problem I will keep you all in my prayers. Tell Darius to reach out when he's up to it." Phil shook Justin's hand and nodded at the ladies.

"You can go back to the office, Sage. I will be there in a few hours after I get Lex settled. Thank you for everything. We all owe you."

"No worries boss. See you soon." Sage gives Justin a slight hug then turned to Alexis, "You behave yourself, Alexis." Sage left Justin and Alexis alone.

The Candidate: Back to Business

Epilogue

Six Months Later

Justin and Alexis sat at the front table helping to celebrate the best night they've had in the last six month. They sat and watched as Darius and Ciara was on the dance floor dancing to their favorite song (Whitney Houston's I Will Always Love You). Justin thought back to six months ago. When Darius was in the hospital fighting for his life. It took almost a week before they got the news that he was going to make it. It took another three week before he was released to go home. He had caught an infection that took a while to clear up.

Ciara was in there for two days. The first time Justin and Alexis went to see Ciara, Alexis couldn't believe her eyes. Ciara face was swollen and he lips were so chapped they were bleeding. She was sleep for the entire first day she was in the hospital. Alexis got out the hospital the next day after the shooting. She stayed with her parents for two days then they all went home. Justin took off from work for almost a week and Alexis took off almost two.

It took more than a week to get everything cleared up with all the damage that Skylar, Harrison, and Danae had going on. Making a deal to get less jail time Harrison came clear about everything. He was filled with just as much hate as Skylar. He was also bitter towards Justin and Darius. Justin because he felt he told WES from him and Darius because Harrison was deeply in love with Skylar, but Darius messed all of that up because he took Skylar away from him. He didn't have any feelings for Skylar, but her obsession with Darius towards the end degraded Harrison.

Harrison told the police that Danae was responsible for all of the prank phone calls Ciara was receiving. It was Skylar that broke into Ciara's house. Both Harrison and Skylar were responsible for the newspaper article about Darius. Harrison admitted they he and Skylar were going to keep at it until he either gotten the company or destroyed the business. Things started to fall apart when he couldn't get Skylar do any more damage to the business. He wanted to continue but Skylar didn't have the time to invest in doing any more damage. Then she stop sleeping with him. She said she was sick of pretended that she was enjoying having sex with him. This hurt his ego so Harrison wasn't in the mood when Alexis came over to the house. He she all he could hear was Skylar's voice telling him that Darius was better in bed then he was and that she wasn't going to never have sex with him again.

Harrison said that when Alexis came by to see him he was out of his my with the unfairness that Justin and Darius had brought to his life. He said he would have let her go, but Alexis got in one more jab about WES so he lost it and hit her on the back of her head with a lamp. He didn't plan on killing Alexis until that final time when Skylar came over. He thought he would be able to talk Skylar to moving back to Florida. He was going to leave Alexis in the basement until they left then he was going to let her go.

He told the police Skylar always had something sintered in mind for Ciara. Justin was right about the plans Skylar had of killing Darius, Ciara, Harrison, and Danae then killing herself. She had left a letter on the dresser stating that why they all had to die. She said Danae had to die because she interfered with her relationship with Darius when they were in Florida. She said Danae was the reason why Darius decided to come back to Michigan. She encouraged him so Skylar and Danae relationship was strained after that. She said that Harrison had to die because he was a weak pathetic fool who would never have made it in the business world. He didn't keep his promise to make sure he ruined Darius' career. Ciara was the homewrecker that needed to be taught a lesson. She needed to know she had to pay with her life for stealing another woman's husband. Finally she and Darius story would end like Romeo and Juliette.

"Hey watch it young lady." Justin was broken out of his memories when Alexis tapped him on the arm.

"What are you thinking about?" I've been talking for the last few minutes, but you haven't heard a word I said."

"I was just thinking about all the drama that has been a part of our lives over the last six months."

"Well, all of that is water under the bridge now. Our best friends will be getting married in less than a month and we're going to be Godparents."

"It amazing. DK has come a long way."

"They both have. Seeing them so much and love with a baby on the way is more than we could have ever expected."

"Yeah I know. The best of all is Sage will be the ceremony. She still talking about the cruise Darius sent her on two months after she came back."

"Well she was the reason why they figured out a way to get in the house during the standoff. She was their Shero."

"What are you guys whispering about?" Ciara asked tired from her dancing.

"Everything that happened over the last six months." Justin answered.

"Tonight isn't the time for that. Those people are out of our lives. It's time for a new chapter in our lives."

"Ciara this is our new chapter. We have so much to be grateful. This is the last time I'm going to say this, I kind of feel sorry for Harrison." The other three people at the time looked at Alexis liked she lost her mind.

"You can't be serious." Justin said.

"Yes he's going to spend the next fifteen years of his life in prison. All the money in the world didn't change that fact."

"He is where he belongs. Now let make a toast. To family."

"To family." The others spoke.

"Let us all be as happy as we are today for the rest of our lives. Enjoy the rest of this weekend because once Monday gets here we all are going to have to get **BACK TO BUSINESS**.

The Candidate: Back to Business
Discussion Questions

Listed below are discussion questions your book club or reading group may be interested in discussing:

1) Since Darius was away so long do you think Justin was wrong to appoint him as CCO of WES?

2) Do you think Justin had too much faith when it came to Darius?

3) What do you think about the friendships between Justin and Darius and Alexis and Ciara?

4) Do you feel it was unfair of Darius not to tell Justin and Alexis about his time spent in Florida?

5) What do you think about the Harrison character?

6) Do you think Darius was the blame for the unhealthy feelings Skylar had for him?

7) Was there something that Justin could have done differently before he appointed Darius as CCO?

8) Do you think Alexis felt threaten by the relationship between Justin and Darius?

9) Do you think it was right for Ciara to cut her ties with Alexis when she found out about Darius past?

10) The Justin character tried hard to make everything right with his family and business. Do you think that he was unrealistic?

11) What do you think about the ending of this book?

12) If there is a book three to this series who do you think should be the main character?

Dear Reader,

I hope you enjoyed reading **The Candidate: Back to Business.** This is the second book in **The Candidate** series. I like to keep my readers entertained by writing something that is satisfying and inspirational. Thank you for taking the time out to read this book.

It would be greatly appreciated if you would consider writing a review of this title on Amazon, Barnes & Noble, and/or the author's website at dianacarterwriter.com in the Comments section under Contact Us (located under the More tab). When you visit the website, you will be informed about upcoming events, publishing services offered, and more.

God's blessings,

Diana Carter

You can find me on the web:

Website: www.dianacarterwriter.com
Amazon Author Page: www.amazon.com/author/diana.carter
Goodreads: www.Goodreads.com/dianacarter

The Candidate: Back to Business
Author's Information

Diana Carter started her writing career after taking a personality test many years ago and disagreeing with the results. After talking to the administrator of that test, Diana was encouraged to submit the book she had written for publication. Born was her first book **Broken Promises: Shattered Dreams** which was published on April 10, 2014, by Outskirts Press. This title was later republished by Diana's publishing company, Let's Do This Publishing, LLC (LDTP) in 2019. Along with the first book in the **Broken Promises** series, books two and three and the first book in the **Dark Revenge** series were also republished by LDTP. See the list of other titles written by Diana in the front of this book.

Diana has a passion for writing fictional stories that will not only entertain her readers but also have a lasting impact. She loves to write and looks forward to continuing for many years to come. When she takes a break from writing, she likes to spend time with her children, grandchildren, bowl, read, and tutoring disadvantaged adults.

You can find additional information on Diana's website at www.dianacarterwriter.com, or by checking out her Amazon page at: amazon.com/author/diana.carter or if you like to personally reach her do so via email at diana.carter44@gmail.com.

www.ingramcontent.com/pod-product-compliance
Lightning Source LLC
Chambersburg PA
CBHW020539080526
44583CB00013B/909